Dr SHANTHA N NAIR

The Holy Himalayas

an abode of Hindu Gods

a journey through the mighty Himalayas

HINDOOLOGY BOOKS

Published by

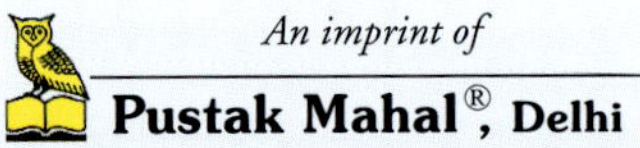

J-3/16 , Daryaganj, New Delhi-110002
☎ 23276539, 23272783, 23272784 • *Fax:* 011-23260518
E-mail: info@pustakmahal.com • *Website:* www.pustakmahal.com

London Office
5, Roddell Court, Bath Road, Slough SL3 OQJ, England
E-mail: pustakmahaluk@pustakmahal.com

Sales Centre
10-B, Netaji Subhash Marg, Daryaganj, New Delhi-110002
☎ 23268292, 23268293, 23279900 • *Fax:* 011-23280567
E-mail: rapidexdelhi@indiatimes.com

Branch Offices
Bangalore: ☎ 22234025
E-mail: pmblr@sancharnet.in • pustak@sancharnet.in
Mumbai: ☎ 22010941
E-mail: rapidex@bom5.vsnl.net.in
Patna: ☎ 3294193 • *Telefax:* 0612-2302719
E-mail: rapidexptn@rediffmail.com
Hyderabad: *Telefax:* 040-24737290
E-mail: pustakmahalhyd@yahoo.co.in

ISBN 978-81-223-0967-6

Edition : June 2007

Photo Credits : N.S. Rana, Rajeev Rana, Avinash Sharma, Ajay Lal and Pradeep Mittal

Printed at : Gopsons Papers Ltd., NOIDA

ACKNOWLEDGEMENTS

I would like to take this opportunity to thank people who helped me make this dream come true. Apart from my own resources, the information I have presented in this book and the photographs displayed have been obtained from guides, people who visited these places, ashrams, public institutions, travel guides and also from websites. The photographs in particular have been sourced from websites.

As it is not possible to thank each of them individually, I take this opportunity to express my gratitude and thanks to each and every individual and each and every source of information that has helped me with the required details and photographs. It is my earnest wish that this book will benefit at least a few, if not all.

Even with all this help, the information presented here about the enchanting Himalayas and its most important sacred places forms only a drop in the ocean.

I owe my gratitude to my husband Mr K C N Nair for all his invaluable help, suggestions and guidance. I would like to thank my son Uday G S and my daughter-in-law Roopa for their assistance and co-operation.

Special thanks to my sweet little grandson Pranav Shankar, who has contributed in his own way by enabling me to complete this work within a short span of time.

PREFACE

The Holy Himalayas — an abode of Hindu Gods, was never meant to be a book. When my husband and I got an opportunity to go on a pilgrimage to Rishikesh and its surrounding places, my joy knew no bounds. Even though I had visited some of these and other places in the north about twenty years ago, I was overwhelmed with ecstasy at the prospect of visiting these lovely places again.

The sacred and majestic Himalayas have always enchanted me since childhood. The more I got acquainted with the holy and beautiful places there, the more thrilled I felt. So, you can easily imagine the state of my mind when my husband and I undertook this trip on the initiative of our dear son.

This writing originally began as a diary of the events of our twenty-day tour to the extreme north of India, the places we visited, how we visited them, where we stayed, our daily routine, and our impressions.

When I finished writing the diary, though, I found that it contained some information that would be useful to those wishing to visit the Tapo Bhoomi and Dev Bhoomi. So, I decided to convert my jottings into a small book titled Reminiscences of My Journey, by avoiding some portions of the diary I found very personal and which would not be of any interest to the others.

Later I found the contents to be very limited for a book. Therefore, I collected more information about the Himalayas as a whole, and some of the other holy and bewitching places there that we could not visit. Finally, this humble book, The Holy Himalayas, emerged.

This book has two parts. The first gives a brief idea about the Himalayas in general, their importance, evolution, divisions, major peaks, sanctity, some hill stations there, important glaciers, rivers, the climate, vegetation and wildlife, the people, adventure sports, and the transport facilities available there.

The second part of the book has thirteen chapters and deals with the location, description, and significance of the places of religious and spiritual importance like Rishikesh, Haridwar, Panch Prayag, the Char Dhams, namely Kedarnath, Badrinath, Gangotri and Yamunotri, Hemkund Saheb, the Valley of Flowers, Mata Vaishno Devi temple, Amarnath, Mount Kailash and Mansarovar. A few photographs of these places are also presented here.

In a humble way, I have tried to give a glimpse of the towering Himalayas in general and the Indian Himalayas in particular in the first part, and about a few sacred places and temples across the mighty Himalayas in the second part.

However, the information and data given in this book are mainly from secondary sources, although primary sources do find some place.

Readers will therefore have to bear in mind the limitations of secondary sources of information and data. There is also variation in the statistical information available from different sources. For example, relating to the heights of the mountains in the Himalayas, the distance from one place to the other and so on. At best, these can be taken only as approximations and not as accurate figures.

Neither do I claim any originality for my work (since all that I have done here is to represent the information I collected) nor do I consider my work scholarly. I shall feel greatly honoured and more than satisfied if this effort is useful to anyone or induces anyone to undertake a trip to the bewitching and holy spots of the Himalayas, since my intention is only to share my joy with as many readers as possible and give at least an outline of the most spectacular monument on earth, the Himalayas.

However, no amount of information, either through word of mouth or by writing can equal or come anywhere near the mystic experience one gains and the ecstasy one feels by travelling through these places of immense natural beauty, and by visiting spots of legendary and historic importance.

The more one explores, the more interesting and vast the Himalayas become. One has to actually see it to believe its magnificence. I wish that everyone gets a chance to visit not only the places included here, but also other places in the Himalayas at least once during their lifetime, as this is a lifetime's experience. I hope this book enables children to get some idea of the enchanting Himalayas. I also hope it is of some help to pilgrims who happen to visit these places for the first time.

Happy pilgrimage…

—Dr Shantha N Nair

PART-I

THE HIMALAYAS

PART-II

SACRED PLACES IN THE HIMALAYAS

PART I

THE HIMALAYAS

AN ABODE OF
HINDU DIVINITY

***Himalayas*—the abode of snow, *Giri Raj*—the monarch of all mountains, is the mightiest, youngest, highest, most inspiring, amazing, and incredible fold mountain chain in the world.**

The Himalayas are called fold mountains because parallel ridges are found here. The towering Himalayas are nature's most magnificent monument on earth. It is the youngest mountain range in the world being only 40 million years old. It is the loftiest mountain chain on earth. It is considered to be the jewel of the world and is undoubtedly the most enchanting gift of nature to mankind. For mankind the mountain has always been shrouded in mystery. There are places here that are still unexplored.

The snow-bound, inspiring, serene, and awesome Himalayan mountains crisscross India, Pakistan, Nepal, Bhutan, Tibet and China. The Indian Himalayan range covers the entire northern sub-continent of India and spreads over its northern parts covering five major areas: Jammu and Kashmir, Himachal Pradesh, Uttaranchal, Sikkim, and the northeastern states of Assam, Nagaland, Tripura, Meghalaya, Manipur, Mizoram, and Arunachal Pradesh. It forms a broad, continuous arc for nearly 2500 kms from east to west, with an average width of 200 kms along the northern fringes of the Indian sub-continent from the bend of the Indus River in the northwest to the Brahmaputra River in the east covering about 230,000 sq miles (595,000 sq kms). In the north–south direction it has an average width of 320 to 400 kms. It rises steeply from the Gangetic Plain. The Tibetan Plateau is located north of this mountain range.

But for the Himalayas, the rain clouds from the Indian Ocean would have passed over to the north—to Central Asia—and the Indian sub-continent would have become a burning desert. The Himalayas also bar the cold winter winds from further north, although a part of these winds cross over to India, resulting in the northeastern monsoon.

The Himalayan ranges have nine out of the ten highest peaks in the world. Five of them are: Mount Everest, Kanchenjunga, Annapurna, K2 (also known as Godwin Austin) and Nanga Parbat. There are nearly 14 peaks of an average of 8,000 metres (26,000 ft), and 30 peaks over 7,620 metres (25,000 ft) besides hundreds of summits of over 23,000 feet. The world's tallest mountains, the Himalayas on an average are more than 5 miles above sea level.

These mountain ranges are always covered by snow and therefore the name Himalayas, meaning '**abode of snow**'. The tallest peak in the world is Mount Everest, about 8,850 metres (29,035 feet) above sea level.

Importance

With varying topography, the gorgeous mountain ranges of the Himalayas are remarkable for their great height, complex geological structure, majestic, lofty, and awe-inspiring snow-capped peaks reaching the sky. Imposing glaciers, deep, gushing, turbulent and thundering holy rivers, natural hot springs, and cascading waterfalls seem to welcome everyone. The deep, dense and lush green forests, flower-bedecked

beautiful, large, low-lying valleys and meadows in high mountain ranges, barren cold deserts, and breathtaking landscapes with lovely and outstanding trekking routes, rich vegetation with a variety of flora and fauna look truly enchanting.

The Himalayas are also endowed with rich cultural heritage, historical, geographical, religious, legendary and mythological importance, spiritual wealth and last but not the least, lovely people.

It is one of the most beautiful places on earth with nature's bounty at its peak, with a spiritual history and mystic atmosphere beyond any comparison, human understanding and expression, leaving one speechless with a tremendous feeling of awe and admiration.

The Himalayas have lured people to this region since ancient times. References about the Himalayas are found even in the **Rig Veda**, the oldest scripture in the world. The Himalayas mean different things to different people. For sages, saints and seekers, it is a spiritual centre beyond comparison. Since time immemorial, ascetics have climbed the great heights in search of peace and wisdom.

The Himalayas are the most sacred and revered mountain ranges of pilgrimage. For tourists, it is a place with the most exotic and picturesque holiday resorts. For thrill seekers, it is the hotbed of many adventure sports. Being the highest mountain range in the world, it has attracted mountain climbers and trekkers. To nature lovers, it is a paradise on earth.

□□□

EVOLUTION OF THE HIMALAYAS

Shivalik Ranges

Himalayan Peaks from Binsar

The history of the Himalayas makes fascinating reading. Its evolution can be traced back to the Jurassic era.

About 250 million years ago, there was a single super-continent on earth called **Pangea.** A large ocean surrounded it. Some 200 million years ago, during the Middle Permian period, this landmass began to split into two. One of them was **Eurasia** (also called Angara) in the northern hemisphere and the second one was **Gondwanaland** in the southern hemisphere. These landmasses began to deposit large quantities of sediment into the shallow sea of Tethys, stretched along the latitudinal area presently occupied by the Great Himalayas.

Gradually, the landmass that is now India broke away from Gondwanaland and floated across the earth's surface. India, a large island, was separated from the Asian continent by the vast ocean, the **Tethys Sea.**

During the movement of the earth's crust, or plates, known as the **Continental Drift,** a theory developed by the German meteorologist, **Alfred Wegener,** the Indian sub-continent began moving northwards towards the main land and hit the Eurasian continental plate. The two continents joined again at the point now known as the **Indus-Yarlung zone.** As it hit the Asian continent, the hard volcanic rocks of India were thrust against the soft sedimentary crust of Asia. This uplifted the seabed and raised the deposits laid down in the shallow Tethys Sea. The history of the emerging mountains started around 70 million years ago, during the period called the **Upper Cretaceous period.** With the collision of the two landmasses, the shallow seabed folded rapidly, was raised into ridges and valleys, and pushed upwards to form the great Himalayas.

About 65 million years ago, during the Eocene period, the bed of the sea began to rise up further, and the sea retreated. The seabed was elevated and the highest mountain ranges in the world, **THE HIMALAYAS,** emerged.

During the middle Miocene period, around 25 million years ago, the low Shivalik ranges came up. From then onwards, mountain ranges began to appear periodically as the Indian plate continued to push the Eurasian plates. The rising of the Himalayas was a gradual process. In this process, the Trans-Himalayan range came first; then to the south, the high Himalayan ranges emerged. At its highest points, the ancient crystalline rock that formed the bottom layers of the sediments of the sea is still found.

Later, the **Shivalik** and **Garhwal Himalayas** sprang up. Evidence for these theories is found in the fossils of the sea animals discovered at a height of 8,000 metres (26,000 ft.) and above.

With the help of GPS (Global Positioning System, a device to measure the minutest changes), it has been proved scientifically that even today, the Indian plate is moving northwards at the rate of about 2 cms every year. Due to this, the Himalayas are growing at the rate of one to two cms every year. Indeed, Mt. Everest has risen around 8.2 metres in the last 100 years. This indicates that the Himalayas are not yet stable; therefore, frequent earthquakes are witnessed here from time to time.

□□□

THE GREAT HIMALAYAN RANGES & PEAKS

Rohtang Pass in Pir Panjal Range

Shivalik Range

Mt. Kanchenjunga (Himadri Range)

Dhaula Dhar Range beyond Dharamshala

The Himalayas are made up of three parallel ranges. From north to south, the greater (or higher) Himalayas are called the **Himadri.** The lesser or middle (inner or lower) Himalayas are the **Himachal,** and the outer (or sub-Himalayas) are named the **Shivaliks.** Collectively these are known as **the Great Himalayan Ranges.**

With major peaks, the greater Himalayas or the Himadri is the highest mountain range in the world. It extends along the northern frontiers of India, Pakistan, Nepal, Bhutan, and Myanmar. It is the highest zone, consisting of snowy peaks, with an altitude of about 4,575 metres to 6,100 metres and about 24 kms (15 miles) width. It contains three highest mountains on earth. They are **Mount Everest, K2 (Godwin Austin)**, and **Kanchenjunga.** To the north of the Great Himalayas lie the Zanskar, Ladakh, and Kailash ranges. On the Tibetan side is the Karakoram Range. Many major mountains of the Himalayan ranges are located in India. The highest mountain in the Indian Himalayas is **Kanchenjunga.**

The lesser Himalayas border the Great Himalayan Range on the north and the Shivalik or outer southern Himalayan ranges in the south. It is the middle section of the Himalayan ranges and lies across north Pakistan, north India, Nepal, and Bhutan. In India, it lies across northwestern India in Himachal Pradesh, Uttaranchal, Sikkim, and Arunachal Pradesh. It varies from about 1,830 to 3,050 metres (6,000 to 10,000 ft) in height and 40 to 80 kms (about 50 miles) in width. It consists of high ranges like Nag Tibba, Dhaula Dhar, and the Pir Panjal. There are hill stations such as Shimla and Darjeeling. The ranges are covered with forests and fertile valleys. Except for Srinagar, Kangra, Kathmandu, and hill stations like Shimla and Darjeeling, the region is moderately populated. One can see numerous gorges and rugged mountains in this region.

The outer or sub or southern Himalayas with smaller peaks is the southernmost, lowest zone. It extends west–northwest for more than 1,600 kms (1,000 miles) from the Teesta River through Nepal across northwestern India and into northern Pakistan. It includes the Shivalik range foothills and the narrow plains at the foot of the Himalayas. The altitude here is about 900 to 1,500 metres with only 16 to 48 kms (10–30 miles) width. The width gradually narrows from about 48 kms in the west until it almost disappears in eastern India. It lies between the lesser Himalayas and the Indo-Gangetic Plain. The **Nanda Devi** with a height of 7,816 metres, the highest peak in India, is located here. There are many long and flat-bottomed valleys called Duns that are spindle-shaped. The Tarai and Duars plains are towards the south of the foothills.

Karakoram Range

Besides these three ranges, there is also the Trans-Himalayan—the northernmost range. It is also called the **Tethys** or **Tibetan Himalayas.** It is located on the Qinghai-Xizang plateau in southern Tibet. This Trans-Himalayan range merges with the Great Himalayan Range on the western Karakoram Range. It has an average altitude of 4,250 metres. It is about 1,000 kms (600 miles) long and 225 kms (140 miles) wide at the centre, narrowing to a 32-km (20 miles) width at the east–west end. It encompasses the valleys of the rivers rising behind the Great Himalayas.

The **Karakoram Mountain Range** contains 96 of the world's 109 peaks over 24,000 feet. From west to east, the Himalayas can be classified into the western, central and eastern Himalayas. Politically the divisions are: the Indian, the Nepalese, and the Tibetan Himalayas. The Tibetan Himalayas are beyond the main Himalayan range and located in the Trans-Himalayan region. Tibet is called the Roof of the World being the world's highest plateau. Nine of the fourteen highest peaks in the world are located in Nepal. Mt. Everest is one among them. Three-fourths of the land area in Nepal is covered by the Himalayas.

FAMOUS PEAKS

Mount Everest

It is the highest peak in the Himalayas with a height of 8,850 metres (29,035 ft) above sea level. However, its height varies depending upon the extent of snowfall on its peak. This mountain is named after **Sir George Everest**. It lies on the borders of Tibet and Nepal. The north of Mt. Everest is in the Tibetan side and the southern side is in Nepal. Mount Everest is known by different names in different regions. It is known as **Sagarmatha** in Nepal, and **Quomolongma** in Tibet. After three decades of attempts, Edmund Hillary and Tenzing Norgay conquered Mt. Everest on 29th May 1953. Since then, many climbers have scaled the peak through various routes.

Kanchenjunga

K2 or Austin Godwin

This is the second highest mountain peak in the world with a height of 8,611 metres (28,250 ft.). It is located in the Karakoram Range on the border between India (J&K) and China. The Karakoram Range extends to 480 kms. It is held by China in the north, India in the east and Pakistan on the west. It is called **Qogir Feng** in Chinese. Locally it is known as *Chogori*, meaning '**the great mountain**'. It is supposed to be the most dangerous mountain in the world for climbers. Up to a height of 6,000 metres, it is rocky and beyond this, it is completely an ocean of snow. It is named after **Henry Godwin Austin**, an explorer. Its other name K2 is taken from the first letter of Karakoram and the number 2 indicates it is the second peak to be conquered.

Kanchenjunga

This is the third highest peak in the world and is located on the Indo-Nepal border. Its altitude is 8,598 metres (28,169 ft). It covers around 7,000 sq kms. It is also known as **Kanchendzonga**, **Kanchendzo-nga**, and **Kanchanfanga**. In the local language, '*Kanchenjunga*' means '*the five treasures of snow*'. This refers to its five summits that are all above 8,000 metres. The five peaks are yet to be explored. It is said that this mountain peak is more dangerous and hard to explore than Mt. Everest. The people of Sikkim consider this mountain sacred and pray to the deity enthroned on the summit.

K-2 (Austin Godwin)

Makalu (top)
Nanga Parbat (middle)
Annapurna (bottom)

Lhotse

This is the fourth highest peak in the world at 8,516 metres. There are two other peaks here—**Lhotse Shar** towards the east of Lhotse and **Nuptse** towards the west. Lhotse is located on the border between China and Nepal. Its east – west crest is located to the south of Mt. Everest. The summits of both the mountains are connected by a ridge.

Makalu

This is the fifth highest peak in the world. This is an isolated peak located 14 miles east of Mt. Everest. Located on the China-Nepal border, Makalu is 8,463 metres high and is like a pyramid with four sharp ridges. **Chomolonzo** at 25,650 ft. is a subsidiary peak of Makalu towards the north.

Cho Oyu

Cho Oyu means the '**Turquoise Goddess**'. This is the sixth highest mountain in the world. Located in eastern Nepal-Tibet border, it has an altitude of 8,210 metres. It lies towards the west of Mt. Everest and Lhotse. The other name of Cho Oyu is **Jobodbuyag**.

Dhaulagiri Mountain

With an altitude of 8,201metres, this is the seventh highest mountain in the world. Dhaulagiri means '**white mountain**'. Along the main peak there are several other pyramidal shaped peaks. Four of them are above 25,000 ft. It is also called **Dhalwalgiri Mountain**.

Manaslu

It is located about 40 miles east of Annapurna, which is the tenth highest peak. Manaslu is at an altitude of 8,156 metres. This is the eighth highest mountain in the world and is located in Nepal. Manaslu derives its name from the Sanskrit word '**Manasa**.' The other peaks around this region are Manaslu north (7,154 metres), Dakura (7,837metres), Himal Chuli (7,864metres), and Manaslu east (7,894 metres).

Nanga Parbat

Nanga Parbat or '**naked mountain**' is the ninth highest mountain in the world at 8,126 metres (26,600 ft.). It is in the Karakoram Range in Pakistan. The mountain has sharp edges that do not hold much snow. This gives the mountain an unclad appearance, therefore the name Nanga Parbat or naked mountain. Sherpas call it '**The Man Eater**' or '**the Mountain of the Devil**'. It has three faces – the Rakhiot, Diamir, and Rupal.

Annapurna

This is the tenth highest mountain on earth and is located in central Nepal. It has an altitude of 8,091 metres. It consists of Annapurna south face (7,219 metres), Gang (7,647 metres), Gangapurna (7,455 metres), Annapurna-3 (7,555 metres), Annapurna-4 (7,525 metres), and Annapurna-2 (7,925 metres). Annapurna in Sanskrit means '**the Goddess of food**' or '**the provider**'.

SACRED PEAKS

These are some of the Himalayan peaks that are not as high as the ones mentioned earlier. Not just the Hindus, people of other religions also consider them sacred.

Kinner Kailash

Neelkanth

Nanda Ghungti

Trishul

Nanda Devi, with a height of 7816 m, is the highest peak in Dev Bhoomi. It is worshipped like a Goddess in Garhwal and the devotees undertake arduous journey through Roopkund and Homekund to participate in Nanda Devi Raj Jat Yatra, every 12 years.

Chaukhamba is a four-cornered peak at the height of 7138 metres.

Trishul, with a height of 7120 metres, is shaped like the trident carried by Lord Shiva.

Neelkanth (6597 metres) is guarding the holy shrine of Badrinath like a vigilant sentinel.

Bhagirathi Peaks (6676 metres) remind us of King Bhagirath's penance.

Nanda Ghungti is another sacred peak with a height of 6309 metres.

Shivling (6543 metres) is associated with Lord Shiva as the name suggests.

Kinner Kailash has a height of 6050 metres and considered sacred by both Hindus and Buddhists.

□□□

SANCTITY OF THE HIMALAYAS

Since time immemorial, the mighty Himalayas have been revered as the abode of divinity. The Himalayas are sacred for five of the ancient Asian religions of the world—*Hinduism, Buddhism, Jainism, Sikhism,* and the *Bon tradition* of Tibet.

Hindus consider the entire Himalayan mountain range as divine. Mt. Kailash particularly is considered to be the abode of Lord Shiva and his consort Goddess Parvati. Ganga and Yamuna are considered by Hindus as the most sacred rivers. It is the home for a major Hindu pilgrimage. In the Bhagavad Gita, Lord Krishna says, "Among the mountains I am the Himalayas."

Bhairav at Kedarnath

Kye Monastery, Ladakh

To **Jains**, Mt. Kailash is the spot where Rishabhanath, the first of the 24 Teerthankaras, achieved Enlightenment. Shenab, the legendary founder of **Bon**, is believed to have meditated in the Himalayas. **Sikhs** revere Hemkund as the place where Guru Gobind Singh, the last of their ten main teachers, practised meditation in his previous life.

Hemkund

To **Buddhists**, it is the place where the Tibetan monk Milarepa meditated and attained Enlightenment. They worship this sacred mountain as a place of power where their sages, roaming the Himalayan jungles and living in caves, attained spiritual realisation and Enlightenment.

The spiritual grandeur of the Himalayas has attracted saints, sages, philosophers and pilgrims alike for countless centuries. Every hilltop here is considered divine and every stream holy. Spiritual tranquillity has always been associated with these snowy mountains since ancient times. The Himalayan region is full of places of worship and pilgrimage. There are several pilgrimage sites and shrines on ice-clad peaks, valleys, hinterlands and at the foothills of the Himalayas. Most of these shrines are closely associated with ancient Indian scriptures that form the backdrop of Indian culture and ethos.

The Garhwal Himalayas particularly, with Tibet in the north and the great Indo-Gangetic Plains in the south, is endowed with unexcelled beauty and is so spiritually enchanting that it is known as a 'Paradise on earth'. This land, with its indescribable

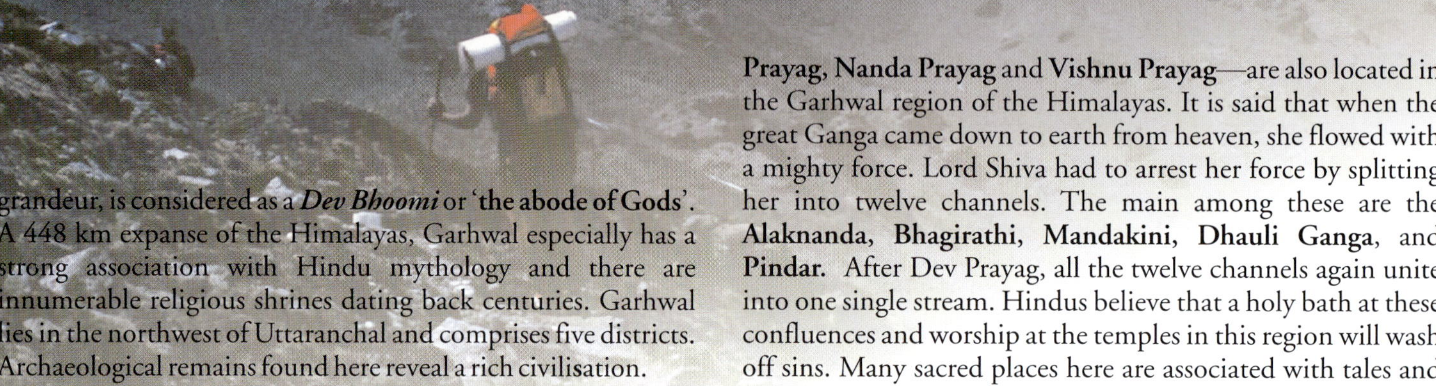

grandeur, is considered as a ***Dev Bhoomi*** or '**the abode of Gods**'. A 448 km expanse of the Himalayas, Garhwal especially has a strong association with Hindu mythology and there are innumerable religious shrines dating back centuries. Garhwal lies in the northwest of Uttaranchal and comprises five districts. Archaeological remains found here reveal a rich civilisation.

The Himalayas house four Hindu shrines popularly known as ***Char Dham*—Yamunotri, Gangotri, Kedarnath** and **Badrinath.** Hindus believe that a visit to all these sacred places and a holy dip there washes off sins and ensures Moksha (freedom from the cycle of birth and rebirth). It is said that these four sacred places should be visited from left to right, beginning with Yamunotri, and thereafter, Gangotri, Kedarnath and Badrinath.

The *Panch Badris* are also located here. They are **Yogadhyan Badri, Bhavishya Badri, Vridha Badri** or the **Old Badri**, and **Adi Badri**, along with the main shrine of Lord Badrinath namely **Vishal Badri**. The ***Panch Kedars*—Madhya Maheshwar, Tunganath, Kalpeshwar, Rudranath** and **Kedarnath** are located here.

The five sacred confluences of great religious importance known as ***Panch Prayag*—Dev Prayag, Rudra Prayag, Karna Prayag, Nanda Prayag** and **Vishnu Prayag**—are also located in the Garhwal region of the Himalayas. It is said that when the great Ganga came down to earth from heaven, she flowed with a mighty force. Lord Shiva had to arrest her force by splitting her into twelve channels. The main among these are the **Alaknanda, Bhagirathi, Mandakini, Dhauli Ganga**, and **Pindar.** After Dev Prayag, all the twelve channels again unite into one single stream. Hindus believe that a holy bath at these confluences and worship at the temples in this region will wash off sins. Many sacred places here are associated with tales and events from the Mahabharata.

The traditional name of Garhwal was Uttarkhand. The Garhwal and Kumaon contain some of the finest peaks of the Himalayas. The high peaks of Garhwal—**Kamet, Trishul**, and **Nanda Devi**—stand majestically here. There are also beautiful valleys and meadows.

High in the Himalayan ranges of Garhwal hills lies the enchanting **Valley of Flowers**, considered to be the playground of fairies and nymphs. Legend has it that this valley is the place from where Hanuman collected the Sanjeevani herb to revive Lakshman, the younger brother of Lord Rama, during the war with Ravana.

The **Hemkund Saheb**, near the Valley of Flowers, is an important pilgrimage both for Hindus and Sikhs. It is believed that Lakshman meditated here to regain his strength after being severely wounded in the war with Ravana.

Neelkanth

Meditation at Dev Prayag

The **Amarnath Cave** in Jammu and Kashmir is supposed to be the sacred cave chosen by Lord Shiva to narrate the secrets of immortality and creation to his consort Goddess Parvati. The temple of **Mata Vaishno Devi** is located in a cave on the Trikuta Mountains in the north of Jammu. Goddess Durga is said to have killed the demon king Bhairav here.

Mount Kailash—Asia's most sacred mountain—stands in a remote corner of western Tibet on the Himalayas. In the shape of a pyramid, this mountain is most sacred to Hindus, Buddhists, Jains and the pre-Buddhist religion, Bon. Hindus consider Mt. Kailash as the spiritual centre of the entire Universe—'**pillar of the world**'—around which everything revolves and where Lord Shiva is seated with his consort Parvati.

Mansarovar is the highest freshwater lake in the world, with varying colours. It lies on the periphery of Mt. Kailash at a distance of 30 kms to the south. It is said that Lord Brahma, the creator, had an insight and then created this lake. The Himalayas are not yet stable; therefore, frequent earthquakes are witnessed here from time to time.

□□□

Bhagirathi at Uttarkashi

GLACIERS

Himalayan glaciers cover a vast area of about three million hectares and comprise 17% of the mountain area. Numbering about 15,000, these glaciers form the main source of water for perennial rivers like the Indus, Ganges, and Brahmaputra, which originate there and form the lifeline of the people along their course.

It is estimated that the Gangetic Plain alone is home to nearly 500 million Indian people. These glaciers also give a tremendous cooling effect to the entire region by influencing the climate. They are responsible for the huge bio-diversity of flora and fauna in these regions.

The **Ladakh** and **Jammu and Kashmir glaciers** are supposed to be the largest glaciers, apart from the polar region. The **Biafo glacier** is located in Ladakh and J&K with a length of 60 kms. It lies on the south-facing slopes of the Karakoram Range.

The **Siachen glacier** is near the Indo-Tibet border in J&K. It is the largest glacier with a length of 72 kms located on the north-facing slopes of the Karakoram Range. It is more than 2 kms wide.

To the east of the Siachen is the **Rimo glacier** group with three glaciers—north, central, and south—located between 6,000 to 7,000 metres. These have almost 700 sq kms of ice that is 100 metres deep at certain places.

Ladakh Glacier

Ladakh Glacier

Thajiwas Glacier (J&K)

Gangotri Glacier

The **Baltoro glacier** in J&K has a length of 62 kms. It is the second largest glacier in the Himalayan region. The third largest glacier in the Himalayas is the **Hispar glacier**. It is also located in Ladakh on the slopes of the Karakoram Range. Its length is 60 kms. The **Nubra glacier** in Ladakh lies on the southern slopes of the Karakoram Range.

One of the Uttaranchal glaciers is the **Bunderpoonch glacier**—an important glacier of the Yamuna river basin at an altitude of 6,316 metres to 6,387 metres. It is 12 kms long and situated on the northern slopes of the Bunderpoonch peak, Bunderpoonch west and Khatling peak.

The **Khatling glacier** is in Garhwal. It is located in the Yamuna river basin at 6,316 metres to 6,387 metres. The **Gangotri glacier** is at Uttarkashi in Garhwal. It originates from the northern slope of the Chaukhamba range of peaks. It is 28 kms long and terminates at Goumukh. The **Chorbari Bamak glacier** in Garhwal is located at Rudra Prayag. It is 6 kms long and originates from the southern slopes of Kedar, Bharckhunta and Kirti Stambh.

The **Dokriani glacier** is a medium-sized glacier of the Bhagirathi basin, with an altitude of 5,600 metres to 6,000 metres. It is 5 kms long. The **Doonagiri glacier** is an important glacier in the Dhauli Ganga system where more than 500 glaciers lie deep in valleys.

The **Tiprabamak glacier** in Garhwal is the longest glacier of the Bhyander Ganga basin in the Alaknanda catchment area. It is 6 kms long. Nearly sixteen glaciers exist in the basin. The **Satopanth** and **Bhagirathi-Kharak glaciers** in Garhwal have an altitude of 3,810 metres to 3,820 metres. These are important glaciers in the upper Alaknanda basin and form the source of the Alaknanda River. **Satopanth** is derived from the word *Sato* meaning 'heaven' and *panth* meaning 'way' or 'path'. These glaciers originate from the Chaukhamba and Badrinath range of peaks.

The **Nanda Devi** group of **glaciers** in the Garhwal includes Nanda Devi north and Nanda Devi south. It is approximately 19 kms long and located in the Rishi Ganga river catchment. These glaciers originate from the Nanda Devi peak. The **Pindari glacier** lies in Kumaon between the Nanda Devi and Nandakot peaks. It is 5 kms long. It is located in Pinder valley. Its altitude varies between 3,600 metres and 5,000 metres. The **Kaphini glacier** in Kumaon is between 6,236 metres and 6,860 metres. It lies to the left of the Pinder valley.

There are also the **Maiktoli glacier, Sunderdhunga glacier, Milam glacier, Ralam glacier** and **Namik glaciers** in Kumaon. Due to global warming, the Himalayan glaciers are receding fast and if the present rate continues, there is likelihood that they may disappear very soon, especially if the earth gets warmer at the current rate. The rapidly melting glaciers will first increase the flow of water in the rivers and cause floods.

But in the course of time, when the glaciers are no more, the water level in the rivers will decline, causing massive economic and environmental problems. As the glacier water flow decreases, the energy potential of hydroelectric power will decrease and this will cause problems for industry and agriculture.

In addition, recession of the glaciers will cause ecological imbalance in the region, besides drying up of the perennial rivers resulting in water scarcity.

It has been estimated that the Gangotri glacier, for example, is receding very fast at a rate of 600 metres over the last 50 years with an average of 20 metres every year since 1990. The reasons are global warming on the one hand and increasing human activities in the Himalayas on the other, together with continuous deforestation by the inhabitants of this region who are very poor and therefore cannot afford alternate sources of energy. Some experts even recommend a ban on trekking and mountaineering to protect these regions from the heavy influx of people.

□□□

RIVERS

The Himalayas also serve as a base for many great perennial rivers with their source in the Trans-Himalayan Ranges. Some of these rivers are the lifelines of India, irrigating vast tracts of land and providing water to millions of people here. Many of the rivers originate from snow-filled glaciers.

Chandra Bhaga River (Lahaul-Spiti)

Sindhu River (Ladakh)

Beas at Manali

Ganga at Haridwar

Yamuna at Mathura

The **Indus** or **Sindhu** River rises in the north of Kailash, near the Mansarovar Lake. It is said that the names '**India**' and '**Hindus**' were derived from *Sindhu*, the name of the river.

The three most sacred rivers for Hindus are the **Ganga**, **Yamuna** and **Brahmaputra**.

- **Ganga** originates from the Gangotri glaciers. At its source, it is known as the Bhagirathi.
- The **Yamuna** flows from the Bunderpoonch glaciers.
- The **Brahmaputra** emerges from the east of Mount Kailash.
- The five rivers—**Jhelum**, **Chenab**, **Ravi**, **Beas** and **Sutlej**—popularly known as '**The Five Sisters**', originate here.

Brahmaputra

Sutlej

Ravi

Jhelum

Spiti

- The **Jhelum** has its source from the spring called Verinag, towards the south of Srinagar.
- The **Chenab** or **Chandra Bhaga River** (the rivers Chandra and Bhaga join to form the Chenab River) flows from the snow at the main Himalayan range in the Lahaul and Spiti district.
- The **Ravi**, and **Beas** originate near Rohtang Pass in Pir Panjal to the north of Kullu.
- The **Sutlej** flows from the west of Mt. Kailash.

The **Spiti** River has its source below the Kuzum Pass. The **Karnali** stream originates from the south of Kailash. The Ganga and the Yamuna with their countless tributaries are intertwined with local myths and legends. In addition to the major rivers, there are innumerable lakes, mostly found at less than 500 metres altitude.

□□□

CLIMATE

Leh city (Ladakh)

Lahaul Valley

Gulmarg under heavy snow

Greenery in cold Himalayan desert

The weather in the Himalayas varies depending upon the altitude and location. It gets colder as the elevation increases and wetter as the elevation drops. The southern foothills experience an average summer temperature of about 30 degrees Celsius and average winter temperature of about 18 degrees Celsius. The middle Himalayan valleys have warm temperate climate of about 25 degrees Celsius and cooler winters.

In the higher parts of the middle Himalayas, one finds cool temperate conditions with temperatures varying between 15 degrees to 18 degrees with freezing winters. At still higher elevation, cold alpine climate is experienced. The summers are cool and winters are severe. Above 4,800 metres (16,000 ft.), the weather is very cold with below freezing temperatures and these areas are permanently covered with snow and ice.

Heavy rainfall is experienced in the eastern parts of the Himalayas. The monsoon rains are mostly from June to September. Due to varying conditions at different altitudes, the temperature and weather changes very quickly in an unpredictable manner. All of a sudden, there can be rains, floods, high winds and snowstorms making the weather quite unpredictable. Further, due to global warming and increasing human presence, the temperature in these regions has increased by 1 to 2 degrees Celsius over the past 20 years.

□□□

Tea Garden (Gangtok)

FLORA & FAUNA

In the Himalayas, both vegetation and wildlife change according to the altitude and climate. A variety of vegetation adds to the charm of this region ranging from dense tropical forests to rain forests and desert vegetation. The four main types of vegetation found here are **tropical, sub-tropical, temperate** and **alpine.**

One finds tremendous bio-diversity too. The different climatic conditions due to varying altitudes have resulted in innumerable varieties of wildlife and thousands of species of flora and fauna. At the foot of the hills where rainfall is less one can see dense, tropical deciduous rain forests of bamboo, oak, and chestnut. In the eastern Himalayas, where there is heavy rainfall, there are dense and evergreen, tropical rain forests with cedars, pines and firs. In the central and western Himalayas, there are dense, sub-tropical and alpine forests. At higher levels, there are temperate forests. Still higher up in the central and western Himalayas, coniferous, sub-alpine and alpine forests are found. These finally give way to alpine grasslands and meadows. Finally, at the Trans-Himalayan region, there is nothing but thin desert vegetation, shrublands and from there onwards there is only a vast expanse of snow, and nothing but thick snow.

Wheat crop

Exotic Sparrow (Ladakh)

Deer (Jim Corbett Park)

Goral

Yak (Ladakh)

Brown Bear

The rugged topography leaves less than 10% of the land fit for agricultural cultivation. The sandy, loamy soils on hillsides and alluvial clays in Kashmir are suitable for agriculture. The main crops here are **rice, corn, wheat, barley, millet** and **potatoes. Apples, apricots, cherries** and **peaches** are grown in Kashmir. **Tea** plantations are found in Darjeeling. Besides, in the Himalayan meadows, there are many medicinal and aromatic plants. In the forest belt of the Himalayas, **oak, rhododendrons, birch, pine** and **deodar** are seen in plenty.

Different kinds of insects, birds, and mammals are seen at different heights. Many species of sheep are found in the Himalayan regions. The largest wild sheep—the **great Tibetan sheep**—lives here. In addition to **mountain goats, brown bear** and **Himalayan black bear, dogs, wolf, wild dogs, hill fox, tiger, leopard, jungle cat, snow leopard, musk deer, Tibetan blue bear, red panther, black necked crane** and other animals are found here.

A Different World

The population of Himalayas is nearly 40 million. Hindus dominate the sub-Himalayan region and middle Himalayan valleys. In the great Himalayan region, towards the north, it is mainly Tibetan Buddhists. While Muslims are seen mostly in western Kashmir, Hindus are seen in eastern Kashmir up to Nepal.

□□□

Kullu Dussehra

One finds a vast variety of tribes and cultures existing here, perhaps due to the isolated living conditions. The population thins out as the elevation increases. The hamlets have diverse local customs, dances, folklore, and distinct lifestyles. There are routes connecting mountain pastures, villages and high altitude passes.

LIFESTYLES

Village life is mainly pastoral and idyllic. Sericulture and sheep breeding are other occupations of the people. Ponies and horses, herds of sheep, goats and yaks graze on the slopes of the hills. Old ladies knit woollen garments all the time, since they are needed throughout the year. People live on the slopes of the hills. The houses are built with clay and wood. The people here are very innocent, far away from modern civilisation, and maintain age-old traditions.

□□□

ADVENTURE SPORTS

Mountaineers in Ladakh

White River Rafting in the Ganga at Rishikesh

The Himalayas offer a wide variety of adventure sports. These include trekking, skiing, mountaineering, rock climbing, para-gliding, jeep and jungle safaris, canoeing, hang gliding, motor rallying, para-sailing, river rafting and so on.

Trekkers to Lahaul-Spiti

Para-gliding at Solang Valley, Manali

Skiing at Auli (Uttarakhand)

The Himalayas undoubtedly are a trekker's paradise. There are difficult and easy, long and short treks. **Trekking** in the harsh climate of the cold deserts of Ladakh, Zanskar, Lahaul and Spiti or in the green pastures of Uttaranchal and Kumaon hills or in the high mountain zones of Nepal is quite thrilling. Nomadic people found in little rural hamlets built in the interiors of the mountains offer help and guidance to trekkers. The necessities of life are also available to trekkers along the way.

River rafting in untamed rivers like the Ganga make the sport truly adventurous. **Mountaineering** and **skiing** on the high slopes of the Himalayas is a dream come true for any skier.

□□□

Shimla

HILL STATIONS

Pahalgam

There are beautiful hill stations in the Himalayas. Some of the famous ones are **Gulmarg, Pahalgam, Sonmarg,** and **Srinagar** in Jammu and Kashmir, **Shimla, Kullu, Manali, Dharamshala** and **Dalhousie** in Himachal Pradesh, **Darjeeling** in West Bengal, **Nainital** (also known as the city of sixty lakes) in the Kumaon Hills, **Mussoorie** (known as the queen of hill stations) in the Garhwal Himalayas, **Gangtok**, the lofty hill which is the capital of Sikkim, and so on.

Srinagar

Dharamshala

Kempty Falls (Mussoorie)

Manali

Bhimtal (Nainital)

Dalhousie (Khajjiyar)

Gulmarg in winter

PART II

Sacred Places in the HIMALAYAS

RISHIKESH

A spiritual town, Rishikesh is located at an altitude of 1,360 ft. It is known as **Tapo Bhoomi** or place for meditation and a place for saints, sages and scholars. It is a gateway to the mighty Himalayas.

It is believed that God Hrishikesh appeared before Rabiya Rishi, who had performed severe penance here. Therefore, this place is called Rishikesh.

Another belief is that it is in this place, at the foot of the mighty Himalayas, that many sages performed severe penance and meditated continuously for such long periods that their hair got matted into locks. So, this place acquired the name 'Rishikesh'. It is also believed that at this place Lord Vishnu vanquished the demon, Madhu. The earlier name of Rishikesh is said to be Kubjamrak.

Location

Rishikesh is located in the Tehri-Garhwal region of the Himalayas. One of the most tranquil places, it is 238 kms by road from Delhi and 23 kms from Haridwar. It has a railway station but many prefer to reach Rishikesh by road, as this is well connected.

Located in the lap of the lower Himalayas, Rishikesh is surrounded on three sides by the Shivalik range of hills. The sacred Ganga flows through it. It is located at the confluence of the Chandra Bhaga and Ganga rivers. All Himalayan pilgrimages begin here. At this spot, the sacred Ganga leaves the mountains and enters the plains. The Ganga is untamed upstream and gushes swiftly through the mountain slopes of the Himalayas. Here it is calm and serene with a steady flow.

The Yoga Capital

Present-day Rishikesh is a small town but a very important pilgrim centre. It is the common gateway to many sacred pilgrim spots in the Garhwal region of the Himalayas, including the **Char Dhams, Panch Prayag** and so on. On the riverside there are many temples, ashrams, yoga and meditation centres. At present this place has become an international meditation centre. It is also known as the '**Yoga Capital of the World**'.

There are many Yogashrams and Ayurvedic treatment centres here. Various ashrams conduct courses on spiritualism, Vedas, etc. In many of the ashrams, no fee is charged for these courses. In addition, free boarding and lodging facilities are provided for participants in these courses, which run into several weeks or even months.

In many ashrams, accommodation is provided to pilgrims for a short period of three to five days at reasonable charges. In some others, donations are accepted for providing accommodation. Free accommodation is also provided for short periods in some places.

The Township

Rishikesh covers an area of 11.20 sq. kms. The approximate population of this place is around 44,500. Of the total population, the floating population comprising pilgrims forms the major component. The town has shops, hotels, restaurants and small business units besides residential houses.

Transport in the form of autos, tempos, tongas and taxis is easily available for commuting within the town.

There are five sections here:

- **Rishikesh town**
- **Muni-ki-Reti or 'sands of the sages'**
- **Shivananda Nagar to the north of Rishikesh**
- **The Temple section of Lakshman Jhoola further north**
- **Various ashrams around Swargashram on the east bank of Ganga across Ram Jhoola**

Many spiritual institutions like Sivananda Ashram (headquarters of the Divine Life Society), Swargashram, Gita Mandir, Parmarth Niketan, Kailash Ashram, Mahesh Yogi Ashram and so on are located here. Most of the ashrams and temples are located on either side of the river Ganga.

Ganga at Rishikesh

Neelkanth Mahadev Temple

Ganga Aarti (Rishikesh)

Kailash Niketan at Rishikesh

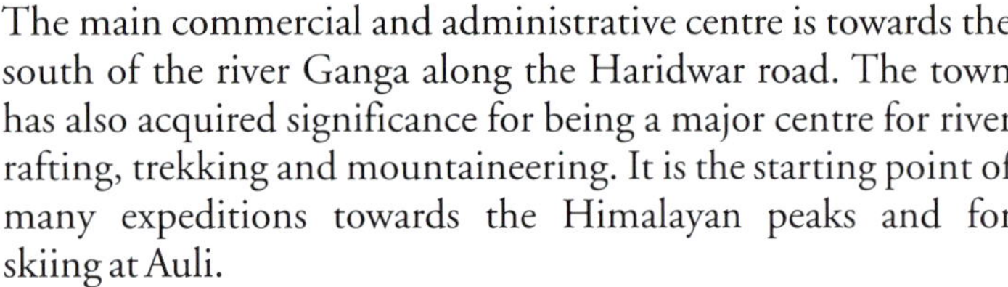

The main commercial and administrative centre is towards the south of the river Ganga along the Haridwar road. The town has also acquired significance for being a major centre for river rafting, trekking and mountaineering. It is the starting point of many expeditions towards the Himalayan peaks and for skiing at Auli.

Ashrams

Rishikesh is famous for its ashrams. Some of them are:

- **Andhra Ashram** run by the Tirumala-Tirupati Devasthanams, Tirupati.
- **Sivananda Ashram,** headquarters of the Divine Life Society founded by Swami Sivananda.
- **Omkarananda Ashram,** also known as **Durga Mandir**.
- **Swargashram** with **Gita Bhavan** founded by Swami Vishudhanand, also known as **Kali Kamliwala** ('the one with the black blanket').
- **Parmarth Niketan Ashram,** one of the largest ashrams with over 1,000 rooms and a big garden, which is the main site and the lead institution for international Yoga festivals.
- Other ashrams include **Veda Niketan, Kailash Ashram, Vedanta Ashram, Vanmali Gita Yogashram, Mahesh Yogi Ashram, Yoga Niketan, Vanaprasth Ashram, Vithal Ashram, Osho's Ashram** and others.

The Famous Bridges

Lakshman Jhoola is a 450-foot long suspension bridge built in 1939 to replace the old rope bridge, 5 kms from Rishikesh on the way to Badrinath. It is believed that Lakshman, the younger brother of Sri Rama, crossed the river here on a jute rope. The old Lakshman temple is on the west bank of the river Ganga. This area is picturesque and very quiet. On the northeastern side of the river are secluded beaches.

Ram Jhoola is a hanging bridge across the river Ganga, also known as **Shivananda Jhoola.** This bridge is made out of steel wires. It is 150 metres above sea level. In addition to pedestrians, two-wheelers are also allowed to ply over it. It is located between Sivananda Ashram and Swargashram.

The Temples

Many temples are located on the other side of Ram Jhoola. These are **Rameshwar Temple, Lakshmi Narayan Temple** and **Gita Bhavan**, with statues and attractive paintings from Hindu mythology. Various chapters from the Ramayana and Bhagavad Gita are inscribed on the walls at Gita Bhavan. Adjacent to the temple, inside the compound there is an ashram. Old, homeless people come and stay here. There are also shops in the campus selling genuine products like crystals, Navaratna gems, rudraksha, etc., on no profit no loss basis. A **Navagraha Temple** is also located in the ashram.

Kailash Niketan, a thirteen-storey mansion with sculptures of all gods and goddesses is on the other side of Lakshman Jhoola. **Lord Venkateshwara Temple** and the **Chandramoleshwara Temple** run by the Tirumala-Tirupati Devasthanams, Tirupati, is located on the Muni-ki-Reti road. **Veerabhadra Temple, Pataleshwar Temple, Bhairav Temple, Someshwara Temple, Kali Temple, Chitragupta Temple, Bhuvaneshwara Temple, Pushkar Temple, Shatrughna Temple and Lakshman Temple** are the other ones found here.

Shiva statue at Parmarth Niketan
Parmarth Niketan (right, top)
Ganga Ghat Temple (right)

Bharat Temple

It is the oldest temple in Rishikesh. Adi Shankara was supposed to have built the Bharat Mandir here around the 12th century. It is located near Triveni Ghat. It is believed that Bharat, the younger brother of Lord Rama, meditated here along with his brother Shatrughna. This temple is named after Bharat, although it is actually dedicated to Lord Vishnu. There are many images associated with Lord Shiva as well. In the inner sanctum sanctorum, there is an idol of Lord Vishnu carved out of a single Shaligram. The oldest statue here is that of Jain sage Mahavira. There is also an idol of Lord Indra on an elephant and a red sandstone Buddha head. In the inner canopy above the idol is a Sri Yantra installed by Adi Shankara. The original temple was destroyed in AD 1398. During a recent excavation, besides two life-size statues of Yaksha and Yakshi, many other statues, coins, pots and artefacts of historical importance were found inside the temple.

Neelkanth Mahadev Temple

12 kms away from Rishikesh, towards its eastern side, is the Neelkanth Mahadev Temple at a height of 5,500 feet. It is a 12-km trek from Lakshman Jhoola and 22 kms by motor road. This is also called the Siddhi Sthal of saints. The temple is located between the hills of Manikoot, Vishnukoot and Brahmakoot. From the mountain above, one can have a good view of the Himalayan peaks, Himalayan forests and the plains below. The temple can also be reached by jeep, car or van. This temple is believed to be the site where Lord Shiva drank poison during churning of the ocean and sat meditating for years. It is said that when Lord Shiva consumed the poison, his throat became blue, hence the name of the temple.

Triveni Ghat

A sacred bathing ghat on the banks of the Ganga, Triveni Ghat is another important place at Rishikesh. This ghat is believed to be the location of the confluence of the Ganga, Yamuna and the legendary Saraswati rivers and is considered an equivalent of Brahma Kund in Haridwar. Many temples surround the ghat. In the early morning hours, people offer milk to the river to feed fish. At sunset, lamps are floated as *aarti* to Ganga Mata.

Rishi Kund

Close to Triveni Ghat, a sacred pond called Rishi Kund is located. It is said that Goddess Yamuna blessed Saint Kubz by filling this pond with the Yamuna's water. The pond reflects the **Raghunath Temple** located close by.

❑❑❑

HARIDWAR

Haridwar means Door of Gods. It is a gateway to the Himalayas.

It is believed that three Gods—Brahma, Vishnu and Mahesh—had chosen to appear at Haridwar.

Pleased with the penance of Raja Shwetu, Brahma appeared before him and honoured him by staying at Brahma Kund, which was later named Brahmapuri after Lord Brahma.

Lord Vishnu set his feet at Har-ki-Pauri, where the holy Ganga touches the feet of Lord Vishnu and this place got the name Haridwar.

Lord Shiva—furious with Daksha Prajapati, his father-in-law, for being the cause of the self-immolation of Sati—descended from Kailash and destroyed Daksha at Daksheshwara, which later became Shivapuri, Neel Parbat and Haridwar.

Ganga at Har-ki-Pauri

Location

Haridwar is spread over 12.32 sq kms. It is situated at the foot of the Shivalik Mountains and is 292.7 metres above sea level. A temperate zone, the great plains of Ganges begin downwards from here. The high mountains of the Himalayas stand majestically on the eastern and western side of Haridwar.

Chinese traveller Huen Tsang, who had visited this place many centuries ago, described Haridwar as the centre of Hindu culture.

The population of Haridwar is around 1,00,000. This place is connected by rail and road. The local transport here mainly consists of cycle rickshaws and tongas. In addition, there are local bus services.

Mythological Importance

Haridwar has been a sacred place for pilgrimage since ancient times. Then called **Mayapuri** on account of the sacrifices of Sati, it is also known as **Gangadwar** and **Tapovan**. Even more ancient is the name **Kapilsthan** for Haridwar, as this place is believed to be the place where the ancestors of Bhagirath were burnt by the curse of Sage Kapila.

Lord Rama's brother Bharat is said to have passed across this area to Rishikesh, where he performed *tapasya*. It is also believed that the Pandavas, on their way to the Himalayas, had journeyed through this place.

According to devotees, Haridwar is one of the four places—the others being Ujjain, Nasik and Allahabad—where the drops of *amrit* fell after it emerged out of the churning of the ocean.

The Ghats

There are five sacred bathing spots in Haridwar: **Gangadwara, Kankhal, Neel Parbat, Bilwa Teertha** and **Kushavarta.**

Har-ki-Pauri: This is the main ghat in Haridwar. Gangadwara Temple is located near this spot. Each night, Ganga *aarti* is performed at 7 p.m. and many devotees throng Har-ki-Pauri to witness and participate in the *aarti*. Lamps and flowers are floated on the river soon after the ceremony. This ghat is named after the footprints of Lord Hari. The footprints are believed to have been impressed on a stone in the upper wall of the ghat.

It is also believed that in memory of King Brithahari, who did penance here and ascended to heaven, his brother King Vikramaditya created stairs that have been given the name *Har-ki-Pauri*.

Kushavarta Ghat: This ghat is located 200 metres to the south of Brahma Kund. It is believed that Lord Duttatreya did penance here. The ceremony for the dead is performed here and the remains of the dead immersed here.

Brahma Kund

Brahma Kund is located in Har-ki-Pauri. A dip in Brahma Kund is supposed to relieve one of all sins. There are many temples in the vicinity of Har-ki-Pauri. The main temple is dedicated to Ma Ganga.

It is also believed that Brahma, the creator, welcomed the Ganga to the earth from heaven with the jar of elixir that ensured immortality. Some drops of the elixir fell into Brahma Kund resulting in added sanctity to the Ganga water here.

Mighty Ganga and Bilwa Parbat

Temples and Ashrams

Like Rishikesh, Haridwar is full of ashrams and religious institutions. It is believed that Yakshas and Devas had the great darshan of Lord Vishnu here. Every 12 years the **Kumbh Mela** and every six years the **Ardh Kumbh Mela** are held here.

Sapta Rishi Ashram is the place where Ganga divided into seven parts, at the request of seven rishis, to flow besides each of their ashrams. **Gita Bhavan** is located on Bholagiri Road. There is a huge marble idol of Lord Vishnu here.

Some of the main temples in Haridwar are:

Mansa Devi Temple: It is located on top of Bilwa Parbat in the Shivalik hills. There is a ropeway and a trekking route to reach the temple at the top. By cable car it takes only 4-5 minutes to reach the top, while trekking takes nearly 45 minutes. It is located at a distance of 1 km from Haridwar. From here, one can have an excellent view of Haridwar. It is one of the most ancient and famous Siddhipeeth.

In this temple, one idol of the goddess has three faces and five arms and the other has eight arms. Mansa Devi is believed to be the wife of Naga King Vasuki and the daughter of Sage Kashyap. Since she was born from his *mind*, she came to be known as *Mansa Devi*. *Mansa* also means *wishes*. So, she is also considered

Ropeway to Mansa Devi Temple

Bhim Goda (top right)
Famous Ganga Aarti at Har-ki-Pauri (top left)

Lal Devi Temple

the wish-fulfilling goddess. To seek her blessings and fulfil wishes, devotees tie a thread on the sacred tree near the temple. Once their wishes are fulfilled, they return to untie a thread from the same tree.

Chandi Devi Temple: Facing the town below, this temple is located at the top of Neel Parbat on the other side of the river Ganga on the eastern summit of the Shivalik range. One of the ancient temples of India, it is also a Siddhipeeth. The main deity is believed to have been installed by Adi Shankara around the 8th century.

According to legend, Chandi Devi—who appeared from the body cells of Goddess Parvati—killed Chanda and Munda, the army chiefs of demon kings Shumbha and Nishumbha, who had captured the kingdom of Indra. After capturing Deva Loka, the kingdom of Indra, the demon kings threw out all the gods from heaven. After killing these demons, Chandi Devi is said to have rested here. This temple is 6 kms from Haridwar. 200 metres away from the Chandi Devi Temple is the Anjana Devi Temple. It is dedicated to Anjana Devi, mother of Anjaneya (Hanuman). By cable car, it takes only 5 to 10 minutes to reach the top, while trekking along the steep climb takes more than an hour.

Maya Devi Temple: It is one of the Shakti peeths. This is believed to be the place where Sati burnt herself to maintain the honour of her husband Lord Shiva. The heart and navel of Sati is said to have fallen in these parts. It is 1 km from Haridwar. Here, the idol of Durga has three heads. There are also idols of Lord Shiva and Bhairava.

Shravan Nath Temple: Here Lord Pashupathinath and Nandi are worshipped. Near this temple lies Pataleshwar Mahadeva.

Pawandham Temple: 3 kms from Har-ki-Pauri, it is a new temple. It has marble idols of gods and goddesses.

Bharat Mata Temple: It is a seven-storey temple in the north of Haridwar at a distance of 4 kms.

□□□

The actual source of the Sacred Ganga is at **Goumukh** from the Gangotri glacier. At this point the river is known as **Bhagirathi.**

PANCH PRAYAG
(FIVE PRAYAGS)

When the great Ganga came down from the mighty Himalayas at the request of King Bhagirath to cleanse the souls of his ancestors, she gushed through with such great force that Lord Shiva had to arrest her in his matted locks from where she flowed downwards into twelve channels, which formed into several tributaries. The main among them are Alaknanda, Bhagirathi, Mandakini, Dhauli Ganga and Pindar. These five confluences form the Panch Prayag that are of great pilgrim importance.

Alaknanda is the main tributary of the Ganga. The Panch Prayag marks the course of the Alaknanda.

Karna Prayag

Dev Prayag

Location

16 kms beyond Badrinath, on the Balakun peak at a height of 3,641 metres above sea level, the Bhagirathi-Kharak and the Satopanth glaciers form the source of the Alaknanda River. At a distance of 10 kms from Joshimath to the south lies **Vishnu Prayag.** Downhill to the south of Vishnu Prayag is **Nanda Prayag.** Further to the southwest 21 kms further downstream is **Karna Prayag.** Below that, 137 kms from Rishikesh is **Rudra Prayag** and beyond 68 kms from Rishikesh is **Dev Prayag.** All the five sacred confluences lie within the state of Uttaranchal. A dip in all the Panch Prayags is believed to ensure salvation for a pilgrim.

Vishnu Prayag

At this place Vishnu Ganga, known after this point as the river Alaknanda, the main tributary of Ganga rising near Badrinath, flows down to meet the Dhauli Ganga River 10 kms from the north of Joshimath. This confluence is dark and mostly in the shadows of the mountain ranges. Located at a height of 1,372 metres, it is 205 kms from Kedarnath. An ancient temple of Lord Vishnu by a pool called Vishnu Kund is located here. **It is said that Sage Narada worshipped Lord Vishnu at this spot.**

Nanda Prayag

On the Uttarkashi road, 190 kms from Rishikesh, lies Nanda Prayag. Here river Mandakini joins the Alaknanda River. A temple dedicated to Gopalji marks this confluence. At an altitude of 914 metres, it is just 22 kms away from Karna Prayag.

Legend has it that pious King Nanda received a boon as per which Vishnu was to be born as his son. But Lord Vishnu had to be born as the son of Devaki and Vasudeva to annihilate the tyrant King Kansa. So to fulfil his promise to Nanda, Lord Vishnu chose to be brought up by Nanda and his wife Yashoda as their son Krishna. This confluence was thereafter named after King Nanda.

Karna Prayag

Twenty-one kms below Nanda Prayag is Karna Prayag where the Alaknanda and Pindar River (which flows out of the Nanda Devi glacier) meet. There are two temples here, one dedicated to **Goddess Uma** or **Durga** and the other to **Karna**, the tragic hero of the great epic Mahabharata after whose name the place is known. It is located at an altitude of 795 metres above sea level.

The forests surrounding this place are believed to be the meeting place of Shakuntala, the adopted daughter of Kanva Maharshi, and King Dushyanta. It is also believed that Ganga and Lord Shiva appeared before Karna in this place. Besides a temple dedicated to Karna, there are temples of Goddess **Uma Devi, Narayan** and **Gopal** here.

Rudra Prayag

Rudra Prayag

137 kms away from Rishikesh, Rudra Prayag is located where the Alaknanda meets the other major stream of Mandakini flowing from Kedarnath. It is about 610 metres above sea level. All around this place there are lakes and glaciers. The temples of **Rudranath**, **Lakshmi Narayan** and **Chamunda Devi** are the important temples here. An important commercial centre, from here Kedarnath is 84 kms and Badrinath 159 kms.

It is believed that to master the mysteries of music, Sage Narada worshipped Lord Shiva, who appeared in his Rudra incarnation, blessed the sage, and granted him his celestial wish to become the repository of classical music. It is also believed that this is the place where Sati was reborn after her self-immolation due to her father Daksha's humiliation of her husband, Lord Shiva. In her new life, as the daughter of Himavan, she did penance here to seek a boon from Shiva to be his wife again. This place is the point where two routes branch off to the holy shrines of Kedarnath and Badrinath.

Dev Prayag

This confluence is located 68 kms north of Rishikesh at a height of 618 metres above sea level. At this point, the Alaknanda meets the Bhagirathi from the Goumukh to form the sacred Ganga. This is the most spectacular of all confluences. High mountains surround this area with low temperature. Ancient stone scriptures are also found here. It is considered the second most important confluence in India next only to Prayag at Allahabad. The place is famous for temples and river ghats.

It is believed that this is the place where Lord Vishnu asked for three steps of land from King Mahabali. Fairs are held here during Rama Navami, Dussehra and Basant Poornima. There are temples dedicated to Badrinath, Kalabhairava, Shiva, Raghuram, Bharata and Hanuman. It is believed that Brahma and Dasharath prayed here and Rama and Lakshman performed yagna here to atone for the killing of Ravana, whose father was a Brahmin. In the ancient temple of Raghunath, there is a 15-ft tall idol of Lord Rama.

□□□

CHAR DHAMS

In the backdrop of the Kedarnath range, at a height of 3,581 metres lies the Kedarnath temple. It is on a ridge of the 23,000-feet high snowy peak of Mahapanth on the Rudra Himalayan range, which is also known as the Panch Parvatas, namely, **Rudra Himalaya, Vishnupuri, Brahmapuri, Udayagirikanth** and **Swargarohini**.

KEDARNATH

It is said that, except for Yudhishtra, four of the Pandavas died on these peaks. It is also believed that Arjuna meditated here to obtain the Pashupatastra. In search of him, the other Pandavas also came here, where Draupadi, after seeing the heavenly lotus Kalyana Saugandhika, requested Bhima to bring her more of these flowers. During his search for the flower, Bhima met Hanuman, the great devotee of Lord Rama, who was meditating here since the *Treta Yuga*.

According to another legend, Goddess Parvati worshipped Shiva here to unite with him as Ardhanareeshwara. Another story says Nara and Narayana, the two sages believed to be incarnations of Lord Vishnu, meditated before a Shiva lingam made of earth at Badri in the Himalayas for a long time. Impressed, Lord Shiva appeared before them. He was happy to grant them any boon. The two sages then requested the Lord to stay on in Kedarnath permanently. Ever since, the *Jyothirlinga* installed itself in Kedarnath.

Kedarnath Ranges

Location

One of the 12 ***Jyotirlingas*** of Lord Shiva in the northernmost part of India, this temple is located in picturesque surroundings on the marshy plain of the Garhwal Himalayas near the top of Mandakini Valley. It is lies in Uttarkashi district in the north of Uttaranchal and is 234 kms from Rishikesh.

During winter, this place is very cold and the ground is fully covered with snow on account of perpetual snowfall. In summer, the highest temperature is around 20 degrees Celsius. This place receives 150 cms rainfall during monsoons. Behind Kedarnath temple lies the samadhi of Adi Shankara who preached ***Advaita Vedanta***, and left this earth at the age of 32 after establishing four *maths* in the four corners of India.

Samadhi of Adi Shankara and Nandi bull at Kedarnath

The Temples

Adi Shankara built the present temple in 8th century AD. It stands adjacent to the site of an earlier temple that was supposed to have been built by the Pandavas in penance after the great Mahabharata war to atone for their sins during the war. Here Lord Shiva stands in the middle of a wide plateau surrounded by lofty snow-clad peaks. The Shivalinga here faces south. Just before the sanctum sanctorum the idol of **Kedar Gauri** is placed facing the west. The inner walls have paintings of deities and scenes from Hindu mythology.

On the outer parikrama, there are statues of **Goddess Parvati**, **Lakshmi**, the **Pandavas** and so on. Outside the temple at the entrance of the door, there is a giant statue of **Nandi** the bull. The temple of **Bhairava** is located at the south on the peak of a mountain. Bhairava is said to guard the temple during winters, when it is closed.

Priests carrying Debjhola at Kedarnath

The temple has a **Garbha Griha** for worship and a **Mandap** for pilgrims. Usually pilgrims visit Yamunotri and Gangotri and perform *abhishek* to Kedarnath with the holy waters from these places.

Legend of the Pandavas

After the great Mahabharata war at Kurukshetra, the Pandavas set out to Varanasi to obtain blessings from Shiva to ensure salvation from sins committed by killing their kith and kin, including their cousins, the Kauravas. But Lord Shiva was unwilling to give them darshan, so he fled from Kashi to Guptakashi. But the Pandavas followed him to Guptakashi. Lord Shiva then went to Kedarnath. But the Pandavas followed him there too. So he assumed the form of a bull and grazed among the cattle. But at dusk when it was time for the cattle to go home, Bhima—the second amongst the Pandava brothers—stretched his gigantic legs across the mountains over the Kedarnath valley to identify Lord Shiva. Except Shiva all the other cattle passed under his legs. Bhima noticed this and bent down to catch hold of the Lord. At once Lord Shiva sank into the earth. But by then, Bhima had caught hold of the back hump of the bull Shiva. This determination of the Pandavas pleased Lord Shiva, so he relieved them from their sins and told them to worship his hump. From that day, the hump of Lord Shiva is worshipped at the Kedarnath Temple in the conical Shiva pinda form.

The Holy Kunds

Behind the temple is the **Amrit Kund**, and the **Ret Kund** is located near the temple. The lake of ice is very near the temple. At a distance from the temple is the **Udak Kund**. In **Hans Kund**, rituals for the dead are performed by dear and near ones. Ukhimath—below at an altitude of 1,311 metres and which is near Guptakashi—is supposed to be the winter home of the deity of Kedarnath. It is also the seat of the Rawals, who are priests of Kedarnath.

The Pilgrimage

The sanctity and importance of the temple in relieving one's sins is described in various ancient Puranas. A pilgrim who goes to Kedarnath from Rishikesh has to pass through several sacred places, including **Dev Prayag**, where the river Bhagirathi from Goumukh meets the Alaknanda from Satopanth, unites and becomes the sacred Ganga. It is one of the Panch Prayags. There is an ancient temple of Rudranath here. The road to Kedarnath then passes through a tunnel, and goes along the banks of **Mandakini** and then to the first important town in the valley by the name of **Tilwara**.

Pilgrims returning from Kedarnath

Rudranath

At a distance of 10 kms from Tilwara is **Agastyamuni**. It is believed that Sage Agastyamuni meditated here. There is one Agastyamuni temple here. Then comes **Kund**, 15 kms from Agastyamuni and 173 kms from Rishikesh. 15 kms from Kund is the town **Guptakashi**, 1,479 metres above sea level. There are two ancient temples here, dedicated to Chandrashekhar Mahadev and Ardhanareeshwara. At a distance of 2 kms from here, the temple of Mathadevi is located. From Guptakashi, at a distance of 30 kms, there is a temple of Lord Shiva at a great height. This is believed to be the navel of bull Shiva. About 1.5 kms from Guptakashi there is a small place called **Nala**, where Goddess Durga is worshipped in the form of Lalita Devi. Around 23 kms from Guptakashi is Rampur, then Sone Prayag, a little village at the confluence of the Mandakini and Sone Ganga. Then one reaches **Triyuginarayan**, situated 41 kms away from Sone Prayag.

Kedarnath is 28 kms from Triyuginarayan. This is supposed to be the mythological venue of the marriage of Lord Shiva with Parvati. An eternal flame that witnessed the marriage burns before the temple even today. Water that flows from the navel of Lord Vishnu falls into the Kund. **Brahma Kund, Saraswati Kund,** and **Rudra Kund** are also here. It is said that in Saraswati Kund a pair of small golden snakes live. The interiors of the temple are quite dark and pilgrims can step inside with the help of a torch.

Tunganath

After a 16-km descent from Triyuginarayan, the pilgrim reaches **Somedwara** and then **Gouri Kund**. This is the trekking base to Kedarnath. There is a temple dedicated to Gouri here. From here, one treks 13 kms to reach Kedarnath temple. Horses, ponies, and dandis are also available for carrying pilgrims.

Panch Kedars

According to legend, Shiva changed himself into a bull when Bhima chased him. Parts of the bull are believed to be in these Panch Kedars, which are considered sacred places of worship.

1. Kedarnath

Here the **hump** of Lord Shiva is worshipped.

2. Madhya Maheshwar

Here the ***Nabhi*** or middle part of Lord Shiva is worshipped. It is 21 kms from Ukhimath and at a higher altitude of 3,289 metres than Kedarnath, on the slope of a ridge 25 kms northeast of Guptakashi. There is a motorable route from Guptakashi to Kalimath. From Kalimath, it is a trekking route.

3. Tunganath

The ***Bahu*** or hand of Shiva is worshipped here. Also said to be the seat of *swayambhu linga*, it is 37 kms from Ukhimath on the way to Badrinath, at an altitude of 3,680 metres. This is the highest Shiva temple among the Panch Kedars and the highest Hindu shrine in the Himalayas. But it is the easiest to reach.

The *swayambhu linga* is a foot high, dark and tilting towards the left. Two smaller temples dedicated to Goddess Parvati and Vyasa are found in a small courtyard. It is located just below the Chandrashila peak on the Himalayas. Ravana is said to have performed penance at this temple, which has many images, including Kala Bhairava, Veda Vyasa, the Pandava brothers and so on.

4. Rudranath

The ***Mukh*** or face of the bull Shiva is worshipped here. The climb to Rudranath is very strenuous, although it is at a lower altitude of 2,286 metres. It is 23 kms from Gopeshwar. One has to walk 18 kms to the temple by foot over high ridges, sometimes even 4,000 metres above sea level. From here peaks like Hathi Parbat, Nanda Devi, Nanda Ghungti, Trishuli and so on can be viewed.

There are many holy kunds near the Rudranath Temple, namely, Surya Kund, Chandra Kund, Tara Kund, Manas Kund and so on. An additional trek of 3 kms leads one to Anasuya Devi Temple. It is believed that at Vaitarani River, the river of salvation that is near this place, the souls of the dead cross when changing worlds. Devotees come here to offer rituals to their dead ones.

5. Kalpeshwar

The ***Jata*** or hair on the head of the bull Shiva is worshipped here as ***Jatadhar***, on the other side of the Alaknanda. It is located in Urgam valley at 2,134 metres. Urgam is a favourite location for sages.

According to legend, Sage Argya performed *tapas* here and created the nymph Urvashi. Sage Durvasa is also believed to have meditated here under the wish-fulfilling tree—***Kalpavriksha***.

BADRINATH

Dedicated to Lord Vishnu, Badrinath Temple is located in the Tehri-Garhwal Himalayan region. It is in the middle of a beautiful valley at the confluence of the Rishi Ganga and Alaknanda rivers. At a height of 10,400 feet above sea level, it is along the left bank of Alaknanda at Narayana Parbat near the hot water spring **Tapokund.**

Legend has it that when Ganga descended to the earth, the earth could not withstand her force. So she split herself into twelve holy channels. Alaknanda, which is one of the most important, became the abode of Lord Narayan.

It is believed that the idol of Badrinath had been thrown into Alaknanda river during Buddhist era and later on it was retrieved by Adi Shankara from Narad Kund and reinstalled by him.

Legend says that Vishnu did penance in this place. Seeing the Lord doing penance in the open place without any shelter, Lakshmi is believed to have assumed the form of Badri tree to provide him shelter from the changing weather conditions. Hence the name Badri Narayan.It is also said the Lord Vishnu identified himself as Nara and Narayana to Narada Muni who did penance here. He is believed to be worshipping these forms of the Supreme God with the Ashtakshara Mantra even today.

Location

Popularly known as the Garhwal Queen, the Neelkanth peak is at a height of 19,800 feet, about 9 kms southwest of Badri and forms the backdrop of the temple. Standing to the left of Narayana Parbat, it changes colour at sunrise and sunset, therefore being called **shining pyramid**. About 8 kms from Badri in the west lie a group of snow-covered peaks called the Choukamba, at a height of up to 6,700 metres. Wild berries or *Badri* once surrounded this place.

Badrinath

Nara and Narayana

It is flanked by the Nara and Narayana range of hills. Nara Parbat is opposite the main temple and Narayana Parbat is behind Neelkanth peak. The river Alaknanda divides the two mountain ranges of Nara and Narayana. It is believed that the *Guru-Shishya* parampara is symbolised here by the two mountain ranges. Nara represents the *Jeevatma*, the individual soul and Narayana represents the *Parmatma*, the Supreme Reality. In the backdrop of the Nara-Narayana range of mountains is the towering Neelkanth Parbat at a height of 19,800 feet. The *poojaris* or priests of Badrinath Temple belong to the Namboodari Brahmin families of Kerala. Here they are known as **Rawal**.

The Main Temple

There is no historical record about the age of the temple. But references to Lord Badrinath are found in ancient scriptures, including the Vedas, revealing that this shrine existed even during the Vedic period. This temple was originally believed to have been built by Adi Shankara. It is also said that at the time of Ashoka this temple was worshipped as a Buddhist temple. It has been renovated several times due to damage caused by avalanches.

The present temple was built two centuries ago by Garhwal kings. It is 15 metres tall and conical in shape. The idol of Lord Badrinath, the main idol here, is of black shaligram a metre high. On the left are a silver Ganesha and Kubera, the God of wealth. In front, to the left, Garuda is kneeling down. A separate Lakshmi shrine is located to the left of the main temple. A temple of Adi Shankara is located just outside the door of the temple. Standing to the right side are the idols of Nara and Narayana. In front on the right is Narada in a kneeling posture. There are 15 idols in the temple complex, including **Lakshmi, Ganesha, Shiva, Parvati, Kubera, Narada, Udhava, Nara** and **Narayana** and so on. All of them are made of black stone. The main idol is that of Vishnu in a meditative *padmasana* posture, on a raised platform, flanked by Nara and Narayana.

The temple has three parts. **Garbha Griha** (sanctum sanctorum) with the idol of Sri Badrinath (the canopy is covered with gold sheet), the **Darshan Mandap**, where *pooja* is performed and which can accommodate a small number of pilgrims only, and the **Shobha Mandap**, an outer hall where devotees assemble for darshan from morning 6.30 am to 12 noon and again from 4 pm till 9 pm.

In the morning, *Mahabhishek, Abhishek, Gitapath* and *Bhargavapath poojas* are performed. In the evening, *Geet Govind* and *aarti* are performed. *Ashtotram and Sahasranama* recitations go along with *poojas*. After *aarti*, in the presence of devotees, the priest removes all decorations from the idol and covers it only with sandalwood paste, which is removed the next day at *Nirmalya Darshan*. This sandalwood paste is distributed to devotees as *prasad*. One special feature here is that all *poojas* are performed before devotees. Badrinath is also known as Vishal Badri and is worshipped as one of the Panch Badris.

Opening and Closing of the Temple

This is decided in consultation with pandits and astrologers. Generally, the temple is opened during the last week of April or the first week of May and the closing day falls during the second week of November. When the temple is closed, the priests perform *poojas* in Joshimath. In November after performing the last *pooja*, the priests leave lighted ghee lamps in the temple.

It is believed that, accompanied by divine beings, Sage Narada performs *pooja* during winter. On the opening day of the temple, *Chaitra Poornima* day, special significance is attached to the ***Akhand Jyoti Darshan***. During winter, the *poojaris* or Rawals move to Joshimath and the *utsava murtis* are taken to Pandukeshwar. These are taken back when the temple reopens after winter.

The Pilgrimage

Badrinath is approachable by road. From Rishikesh the distance is approximately 298 kms. While going from Rishikesh one has to pass through Dev Prayag, Sri Nagar, Rudra Prayag, Karna Prayag, Nanda Prayag, Joshimath, Vishnu Prayag, Gobind Ghat, Pandukeshwar, Hanumanchatti and Devdarshini.

From Kedarnath there are two routes. One is the **Rudra Prayag route** with a distance of 243 kms and another, the **Ukhimath** and **Gopeshwar route**, is 230 kms.

Tapta Kund (a natural spring on the bank of river Alaknanda)

A pilgrim travelling by the first route has to pass through **Gouri Kund, Sone Prayag, Guptakashi, Agastyamuni, Rudra Prayag, Karna Prayag, Nanda Prayag, Joshimath, Vishnu Prayag, Pandukeshwar, Hanumanchatti** and **Devdarshini.** The second route via Ukhimath passes through **Guptakashi, Joshimath, Vishnu Prayag, Gobind Ghat, Pandukeshwar, Hanumanchatti** and **Devdarshini.** The first route is a direct one but less beautiful, as there are no extensive views of the Himalayas along this route.

Famous Places

There are many places around Badrinath worth seeing. Some are:

Tapta Kund

This is a natural spring on the bank of Alaknanda. Narad Kund is a recess in the river forming a pool and the Badrinath idol was said to have been recovered here. These are hot water springs with a temperature of 55 degrees Celsius, which come from beneath the Garuda Shila and fall into the kund. A darshan of Lord Badrinath is preceded by a dip in both the kunds.

Narad Kund and Surya Kund

These are hot water pools. At a distance of 4.5 kilometres to the north, the Vasudhara waterfalls flow down from a great height. At the rear of Badrinath Temple, a large valley opens to the Neelkanth peaks.

Brahma Kapal

The Brahma Kapal is located to the north of the temple. It is a flat platform on the bank of the Alaknanda where Hindus perform rites for dead ones. According to legend, Lord Shiva had cut one of the five heads of Brahma for his immoral behaviour of being attracted towards his own daughter

Ukhimath

Sandhya. Since then, Brahma is referred to as ***Chaturmukhi*** or *four faces*.

Lord Shiva's trishul had the severed head of Brahma and to separate this, Shiva had to visit several teerthas. Finally, the severed head (***kapal***) slipped off from Lord Shiva's hands and fell near the river Alaknanda. Since then, this place has been called Brahma Kapal.

Keshava Prayag, Vasudhara Falls, and Lakshmivan

Keshava Prayag is located at the confluence of river Saraswati, emerging from a glacier about 3 kms north of Mana and Alaknanda rivers. About 8 kms from Badri is the Vasudhara Falls. The Alkapuri glacier can be seen from here. Lakshmivan is 12 kms from Badrinath and 4 kms from Vasudhara Falls. It is believed that Goddess Lakshmi meditated here. 9 kms from Lakshmivan, the Nara and Narayana mountains merge at Chakratirth.

Satopanth Lake

This is 25 kms from Badrinath, at a height of 4,402 metres above sea level. It is the source of the Alaknanda from the Bhagirathi-Kharak and Satopanth glaciers. Satopanth Lake is three-cornered with a circumference of about 1 km. It is named after three Gods—**Brahma, Vishnu** and **Shiva**—believed to be occupying one corner each. This lake has green, crystal clear water.

Alkapuri

Alkapuri glacier is located at the base of Balakun peak, which is 6,067 metres above sea level. It is 15 kms from Badrinath and 3 kms from Lakshmivan. Narayana Parbat divides the glacier of Alkapuri and Goumukh.

Panchshila and Panch Dharas

The five Shilas—**Varaha Shila, Narad Shila, Narsingh Shila, Garuda Shila** and **Markandeya Shila**—are located above Tapta Kund. Pilgrims unable to walk up to Kedarnath have darshan of these shilas and then go for Badri darshan. The Panch Dharas around Tapta Kund are **Prahlad Dhara, Kurma Dhara, Urvashi Dhara, Bhrigu Dhara** and **Indra Dhara**.

Matamurti

This temple is located on the right bank of the Alaknanda near Keshava Prayag, at a distance of 3 kms from Badrinath. The **Maninag Parbat** is located near this temple.

Near this mountain, Yudhishtra supposedly answered all questions put by Yama and brought back all his brothers who had lost their lives because they could not answer Yama's questions. This temple is dedicated to the mother of Lord Badrinath. It is believed that on *dwadashi*, Badrinath visits this temple to have darshan of his mother. It is also believed that couples with no children will be blessed with progeny if they meditate here.

Manibhadra (Mana gaon)

This village is located at a distance of 5 kms from Badrinath. **Ganesh Gufa** (a cave) and **Vyas Gufa** are located here. Near the caves one can see **Bhim Shila**. Vyas Gufa is near Mana village, 4 kms from Badrinath. An Indo-Mongolian tribe inhabits it. This is the last Indian village before Tibet on this route. Vyas Gufa is located near this place on the banks of the legendary river Saraswati. It is believed that Sage Vyasa composed the great epic Mahabharata and Bhagavata Purana here. From here, one can see a natural bridge called Bhim Pul across the legendary Saraswati River and the 122-metre Vasudhara waterfalls. During winter, this place is inaccessible.

It is believed that Shankara met Vyasa Maharshi in this cave and discussed his *Bhashyam* for the Brahma sutras. The rock formation in the cave appears to resemble the orderly stacking of palm leaf manuscripts. It is worshipped as *Vyas pustak*. Near Vyas Gufa, Ganesh Gufa is located. Ganesh Gufa is said to be the place where Vyasa narrated his works and Ganesha wrote them down on the condition that Vyasa would not stop reciting. At this place, the legendary Saraswati and Alaknanda meet and this confluence is known as Keshava Prayag.

Gobind Ghat

It is located at the confluence of the Alaknanda and Lakshman Ganga. An imposing Gurudwara named after Guru Gobind Singh is located here.

Charan Paduka

This is a beautiful meadow. Footprints on a boulder believed to be that of Lord Vishnu can be seen here.

Gobind Ghat

Joshimath

Shesh Netra
This is a boulder with an impression believed to be that of Adi Shesha's eye.

Bhim-Mukund Caves and Bhim Pul
These caves are located just above Vyas Gufa. Below is Bhim Pul, a bridge said to have been made by Bhima from a huge stone to enable his brothers and Draupadi to cross the river Saraswati. The legendary Saraswati is believed to have emerged from a glacier north of Mana, and touches Vyas Gufa. At Keshava Prayag, it merges with Alaknanda and finally meets Ganga and Yamuna at Triveni Ghat at Rishikesh and Prayag in Allahabad.

Lakshmivan, Chakra Teertha and Swargarohan Mountain
Lakshmivan is believed to be the place where Goddess Lakshmi meditated. Chakra Teertha is where Arjuna had taken a bath and received Lord Shiva's Pashupatastra. **Swargarohan Mountain** is said to be the place from where the Pandavas ascended to heaven.

Joshimath
Located in Tehri-Garhwal region, on the slopes above the confluence of Alaknanda and Dhauli Ganga, Joshimath lies at a distance of 47 kms east of Badrinath at 6,150 ft above sea level. Adi Shankara established his first *math* here, known as **Jyotir Math**. After this, he established three other *maths* in the three corners of India.

There are many old temples here. The main temples are of **Narasimha, Vasudeva, Goddess Durga Mata** and **Garuda**. In the temple of Narasimha established by Adi Shankara, there are idols of Badri Narayan, Udhava, Kubera, Chandika Devi,

Rama, Lakshman, Sita and Garuda inside the sanctum sanctorum. One can see statues of Brahma, Krishna, Lakshmi and Anjaneya outside the temple. Outside the temple of Vasudeva, there are idols of Sri Devi, Bhu Devi, Leela Devi, Urvashi and Balaram, besides the idols of Vinayaka, Brahma, Indra, Chandra, Navagrahas and Gauri Shankar.

Adi Badri

When the Adi Badri temple is closed for six months during winter, *poojas* are performed in the Narasimha Temple here. An Amar Kalpa tree grows here. It is said that Adi Shankara attained Enlightenment here. Sage Vyasa also worshipped Goddess Lakshmi here. It is said that one hand of the presiding deity is being weakened gradually and once the hand disjoints, the way to Badri will be closed eternally. Badri Narayan would thereafter be worshipped from Bhavishya Badri.

Panch Badris

Besides the main temple of Badrinath, there are four other smaller Badri temples. All these five Badris are called *Panch Badris*. In each of these Badris, Badri Narayan is worshipped under five different names.

1. Vishal Badri

It is also known as Badri Vishal. This is the main shrine of Badrinath.

2. Yogadhyan Badri

It is closest to the main temple of Vishal Badri and is at a distance of 24 kms from Badrinath and 20 kms from Joshimath. Located in Pandukeshwar—named after the Pandava kings—at a height of 1,920 metres, here the idol of Lord Vishnu is in a meditative posture. A tiny, sleepy hamlet, it is believed that King Pandu—father of the Pandavas—meditated in Pandukeshwar. Since then, the Lord is worshipped here in the form of Yogadhyan. It is also said that after the Mahabharata war, the victorious but emotionally shattered Pandava brothers renounced their kingdom, took shelter here and made their grandson Parikshit the king. It is supposed to be the winter home of Badrinath.

3. Bhavishya Badri

At a height of 2,744 metres, the Bhavishya or future Badri is located amidst thick forests surrounding Tapovan about 17 kms east of Joshimath. It is believed that when evil is on the rise in the world, the two mountains Nara and Narayana at Badrinath will close in on each other and destroy the route to Badrinath. According to scientists, this may come true since Joshimath, the final entry point to Badrinath, is located on an ancient landslide that is sinking gradually. With a barrage that is coming up nearby, this prophecy may come true. It is believed this will be the end of the present *yuga* and the beginning of a new one. Lord Badrinath will then be worshipped here instead of at Badrinath.

Here the lion-headed image of Narasimha is enshrined. To reach this spot pilgrims have to trek beyond Tapovan, up the Dhauli Ganga river. Tapovan valley has sulphurous hot springs and is indeed very beautiful.

4. Vridha Badri

This is the old Badri, located in Animath at a height of 1,380 metres, at a distance of about 7 kms from Joshimath on the main Rishikesh-Badrinath motor road. It is believed that prior to enshrinement by Adi Shankara at Badri, Badrinath was worshipped here and that the divine Vishvakarma carved the idol here and when *Kali Yuga* dawned, Lord Vishnu chose to leave this place.

5. Adi Badri

Adi Badri is the farthest from the other four Badris. It is located at a distance of 16 kms from Karna Prayag. The temple complex has the remains of 16 smaller temples with intricate carvings of which seven are very old. The main temple is differentiated by a pyramid-shaped raised platform with a one-metre high black stone idol of Lord Vishnu. The temples here have flat roofs belonging to the late Gupta period. The **Mana Narayan Temple** is considered to be the most popular one here.

□□□

It is said in the Bhagavata Purana that Ganga manifested herself in the form of a river to absolve the sins of King Bhagirath's ancestors and to liberate their souls.

It is believed to be the place where Shiva received Ganga in his matted locks to arrest her force downwards.

Gangotri is located at an altitude of 3,140 metres above sea level, on the Garhwal hills in the northwest of the Himalayas. It is one of the four sacred Dhams of Hindus.

GANGOTRI

Location

Located near the Indo-Tibetan border, this is the place where Ganga descends. The starting point of Bhagirathi, the Goumukh, is located at a distance of 18 kms from here at a height of 4,200 metres along the Gangotri glacier.

Pilgrims trek up to this sacred spot on foot or on ponies to take a holy dip in the ice-cold water in the belief that it will wash off their sins.

One can visit Goumukh only between June and September. During the rest of the year, the path is covered with snow. The Bhagirathi River gushes out here from a snout in the Gangotri glacier, which is 6 to 8 kms in width, nearly 24 kms in length and situated in the heart of the Gangotri peaks. At this legendary source, the Ganga is called the **Bhagirathi**.

Ganga Mata temple

The Shrine of Gangotri

Along the right bank of Bhagirathi is the shrine of Gangotri dedicated to the goddess. Standing amidst dense deodar forests and rugged mountains, the temple overlooks the thundering river. The Gangotri shrine was constructed in the early 18th century by a Gorkha commander, Amar Singh Thapa. After it was damaged in an avalanche, the Maharaja of Jaipur renovated it in the 1920s.

By November, Gangotri is covered in snow. The temple is near a stone where it is believed Bhagirath worshipped Lord Shiva. The temple is an exquisite 20-foot high structure made of white granite. In this temple, there are many statues of goddesses, including Yamuna, Saraswati, Lakshmi, Parvati, and Annapurna.

Bhagirath Shila is near the temple. The Shivalinga that is submerged in the river here is visible under the water during the early part of winter when the water level goes down. Bhagirathi joins Kedar Ganga at Devghat, which is down below. During winter, the goddess retreats to Mukhaba, located 12 kms downstream.

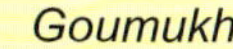

Goumukh

Tapovan

A four-km trek through the massive Goumukh glacier takes one to the high altitude of Tapovan where King Bhagirath did penance. Tapovan is an extremely beautiful spot. It is the foothill of the mighty Shivling peak 6,543 metres above sea level.

It is at this point that Ganga came down from heaven in response to the king's arduous penance. It is said that the king stood on one leg and did penance for nearly 5,500 years! It is also believed that the Pandavas performed Deva Yagna at this place to atone for sins committed by them killing their kith and kin during the Mahabharata war.

At Gangotri, *poojas* are performed for Ganga Mata both inside the temple as well as on the banks of the Ganga. Every year ten Brahmins from Mukhaba are selected in rotation to take charge of the temple. The administration of the temple and the town is in the hands of a local committee made up of five members.

The Pilgrimage

Gangotri is 260 kms from Rishikesh. A pilgrim who starts from Rishikesh to Gangotri has to pass through Tehri and Uttarkashi where there are many temples, including **Vishwanath Temple, Ekadash Rudra Temple, Gyaneshwar Temple, Parasuram Temple** and others. The two most important temples here are the ones of **Lord Shiva** and **Shakti**. Lankachatti is the last motorable point, 235 kms from Rishikesh. The onward journey to Gangotri is on foot, by ponies or dandis. The road is straight and crosses the river Bhagirathi.

In mythology, the river is believed to have been born from the union of the lovesick Sun God Surya and Sanjana, the daughter of Vishwakarma, the chief architect of the world.

Yamunotri is considered the **jewel of the Himalayas.** One of the four sacred Dhams, it is the source of the river Yamuna.

YAMUNOTRI

Location

It is located at an altitude of 3,323 metres above sea level in Uttarkashi district, very close to the Indo-Chinese border. The 6,315 metres high Bunderpoonch mountain glacier lies to the north of the shrine. Behind the temple is a magnificent waterfall that begins from the Bunderpoonch peak and drops more than 2,000 feet into the valley. The left bank of the Yamuna is also called **Kalind Parbat**.

According to legend, this secluded hilly spot was the home of an ancient sage Asit Muni. It has a glacier lake Saptarishi Kund on top, at an altitude of about 14,000 feet (4,421 metres). Further up is the Champasar glacier near Yamunotri. It is 236 kms from Rishikesh and not easily accessible. This place remains cool even during summer and is snow-bound during winter.

Yamunotri Temple

Yamunotri is situated opposite Gangotri. Maharani Gularia of Jaipur built the Yamunotri temple in the 19th century. It was destroyed twice in the 20th century before being rebuilt. The idol here is made of black marble. The main temple is dedicated to Goddess Yamuna. The shrine is in a deep cleft on the western face of the Bunderpoonch peak. This place is worshipped as the source of the holy river Yamuna. But technically, the source of the river is on the Champasar glacier at **Saptarishi Kund**, 12 kms further up.

Near Yamunotri, glaciers are steaming hot springs or kunds. Water rushes out of mountain cavities at boiling point. **Surya Kund** is one of the hottest kunds with a temperature of 190 degrees F. Devotees tie rice and potatoes in muslin and dip them in the hot water spring. When these are taken out, they are completely cooked. These are then taken as offerings to the temple. Near Surya Kund is **Divya Shila**, which is worshipped before worshipping Goddess Yamuna. Divya Shila is a huge rock pillar just before Yamunotri temple. The nearby **Jamuna Bai Kund**, built about 100 years ago, is warm and relaxing and used for bathing.

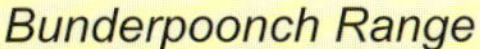

Bunderpoonch Range

Yamunotri Temple

The entire administration of Yamunotri is in the hands of **Pandas**, who hail from village Kharsali on the other bank of Yamuna, near Janakichatti. They are also priests of this temple.

Lakha Mandal

This is a place near Yamunotri on the Mussoorie-Yamunotri road. According to legend, this is where the Kauravas made a lac home for the Pandavas, so that it could be burnt later with the Pandavas inside. Devotees worship here before worshipping Goddess Yamunotri.

The Pilgrimage

From Rishikesh, Yamunotri is 213 kms by road. The important places from Rishikesh to Yamunotri are: **Dehradun**, the capital of Uttaranchal, **Mussoorie**, a famous hill station, **Sayanachatti** and, finally, **Hanumanchatti** located at an altitude of 2,134 metres at the confluence of the Ganga and Yamuna. From Hanumanchatti, a 14-km trek can be covered on foot, ponies, palanquins or horses. Porters are also available to carry pilgrims.

□□□

It is believed that Guru Gobind Singh, the tenth and final Guru of Sikhs, in his former life as Rishi Medhasa, who was believed to be Durga Saptarishi of Markandeya Purana, had selected this place for penance and united with God after prolonged meditation.

Hem means snow and **Kund** means tank. Hemkund reflects its surroundings on the crystal clear waters.

HEMKUND SAHEB

Hemkund Saheb

Location

The high altitude Lok Pal Lake known as Hemkund Saheb or the Lake of Snow is located at 4,329 metres (15,200 feet) above sea level in picturesque surroundings. Seven snow-clad peaks and their associated glaciers of gigantic mountains called Hemkund Parbat encircle it. The glaciers from the **Hathi Parbat** and **Saptarishi** peak feed the lake and a small stream Hemganga flows out of this. The lake water is sweet and filled with lotus flowers. Surrounded by grassy fields, it is an important pilgrimage site for both Hindus and Sikhs. This lake near the Valley of Flowers was discovered by Sikh Hawaldar Sohan Singh in 1930. Along its banks is the sacred star-shaped Gurudwara of Sikhs.

Gobind Ghat (top)

Lakshman Ganga (left)

Glacier on the way(right)

Ghangaria (left bottom)

The Pilgrimage

It is 43 kms from Badrinath. There is a motorable road up to Gobind Ghat, which is 290 kms from Rishikesh and 20 kms from Joshimath. Along this route pilgrims come across **Dev Prayag, Sri Nagar, Rudra Prayag, Joshimath, Gobind Ghat** (set on the confluence of Alaknanda and Lakshman Ganga), **Gopeshwar** (which is very picturesque and has an ancient temple of Lord Shiva and a group of temples without idols) and **Ghangaria**, situated at a height of 304 metres (10, 500 ft) that serves as the base for the Hemkund trek. From here, one treks 5 kms to reach Hemkund Saheb. The journey is very difficult with a steep ascent and one has to travel through snow. From Hemkund, the Hemganga flows and joins Pushpavati River at Ghangaria and becomes Lakshman Ganga, where there is a temple dedicated to Lakshman, the brother of Lord Rama. It is believed that Lakshman did penance here.

□□□

According to legend, this is the place where Hanuman came to collect the Sanjeevani herb to revive Lakshman during the Lanka war.

High in the Himalayan ranges of the Garhwal hills lies the valley of flowers—an exotic valley situated east of Badrinath.

THE VALLEY OF FLOWERS

Location

Located at 3,352 metres (12,000 feet) above sea level towards east of Badrinath, the valley is flanked on either side by majestic snow-capped peaks. With **Rataban** peak in the background, it is a very beautiful, conical-shaped valley spread over 87.5 kms. Formed by retreating glaciers, it is covered with snow from November to May. It is the catchment area of the Pushpavati River, which is known as **Bhyander Ganga,** downstream of Ghangaria. It consists of a glacier corridor 7 kms long and 2 kms wide that descends from **Gouri Parbat.** On the north side of the valley, steep cliffs of about 2000 feet are seen. There are green pastures with clear running streams.

The Fragrance of Flowers

The flowers are usually covered with dewdrops. The air has the fragrance of flowers. Varieties of flowering plants are seen in the surrounding forests, including a large variety of medicinal plants. **Brahma Kamal,** the celestial flower offered to Gods, grows on the higher levels. This valley has the largest collection of wild flowers.

The snow melts from May onwards and till September, the entire valley blooms with exotic flowers. There are 521 species of flowering plants in this valley. For preserving its bio-diversity, the Government declared this area a National Park.

Trekker's camp near Gouri Parbat

Glacier descending from Gouri Parbat

Nag Tal

There are various kinds of birds in the surrounding forests called **Bhyander Valley.** This is believed to be the playground of fairies and nymphs. Himalayan black bears, musk deer, brown bears, snow leopard and other animals inhabit this area. The Pushpavati River emerging from the glaciers around Rataban and Nilgiri ranges cuts through this valley. The major portion of the valley is on its right side. On the left side of the Pushpavati, flatlands are seen. One of them is Nag Tal—a place of venomous serpents and poisonous plants.

Bhyander Ganga

Brahma Kamal

The Journey

This place was discovered in the 1930s by **Frank Smith**—a mountaineer, explorer and botanist—along with **R L Holdsworth.** It covers an area of 87.5 kms and is 6 kms from Bhyander village. The Valley of Flowers is 4 kms from Ghangaria and 19 kms from Gobind Ghat. From Ghangaria, one footpath leads to Hemkund Saheb and another to the Valley of Flowers. Porters and ponies are available to carry pilgrims. From Ghangaria the path is a great ascent to the Valley of Flowers with glaciers, snow bridges and alpine flowers. Wild animals are occasionally seen along the trekking route. **Gobind Dham** is the base for the Valley of Flowers, located in the midst of giant deodars.

□□□

MATA VAISHNO DEVI

This temple is situated in the Trikuta Hills of Jammu and Kashmir. The goddess resides in a beautiful cave in the form of three pindis—Maha Kali, Maha Lakshmi and Maha Saraswati.

According to legend, Maha Kali, Maha Lakshmi and Maha Saraswati pooled their strength and sent a divine child to be born in the house of Ratnakar as Vaishnavi. The child Vaishnavi was extraordinary from her childhood days.

Once she went deep into the forest in search of God. Gorakhnath, a tantrik, sent his disciple Bhairavnath to look for her. To escape from him, Vaishnavi left Trikuta Mountain. Passing through a ravine, she shot an arrow into the earth and water gushed out. This stream later came to be known as the Banganga. Charan Paduka—which has imprints of her feet—is supposed to be the place where she rested. She meditated in the cave at Ardh Kuwari and after nine months was located by Bhairavnath. Thereafter, this cave was named *Garbh Joon*.

When Bhairavnath found her, Vaishnavi blasted an opening at the other end of the cave with her trident. She then assumed the form of Maha Kali and cut off Bhairavnath's head. The head flew up the mountain by sheer force of the blow. It fell at a place where Bhairavnath's temple is located. Bhairavnath was then granted divine forgiveness by the benevolent Mata during his dying moments.

Location

Mata Vaishno Devi Temple is located 61 kms north of Jammu. At a height of 5,100 feet, the cave is 93 feet long and 53 feet high. The present temple is 52 kms from Jammu. The motorable road ends at Katra. From there, the temple is a steep 13 km walk. The trek from Katra takes nearly four hours. But ponies are available to reach the temple.

Bhawan at Trikuta Mountain

Ma Shakti—the Celestial Beauty

A holy Brahmin Pt. Sridhar discovered this holy shrine about 1,000 years ago. He lived in **Hansali village** at the foothills of the Trikuta Mountains. One day as he was grazing his cattle, he met a beautiful child Vaishnavi. She urged him to call all the villagers to a feast. But the feast was not ready even at midday. Suddenly the child came out of the hut and asked Sridhar to call all the guests inside. They went in and enjoyed a grand feast. When all the guests had left, Sridhar called out the child. But she could not be seen anywhere.

Banganga...the journey begins

He then went in search of the divine child. While doing so, he entered a large cave. After a long search, he suddenly saw a light appear. He now had a vision. The child had transformed herself into a celestial beauty with eight arms and was seated astride a lion. She told him she was Shakti and then manifested herself in three forms—Kali, Lakshmi and Saraswati.

The Cave

This cave is very narrow. Pilgrims have to walk through a running stream of Charan Ganga to reach the sanctum sanctorum. At one time only 12 to15 pilgrims are let inside the cave. It is believed that this is the place where the arms of Goddess Sati had fallen. The idols are adorned by silver and gold canopies. Coconuts and red scarves are offered here.

The Pilgrimage

Other shrines located near this temple are: **Bhumika Temple**, 1 km from Katra and **Banganga**, 3 kms from Katra, where water gushed out when the goddess shot an arrow into the stone. The goddess then washed her hair at **Charan Paduka**, which is at a height of 3,380 feet and about 1.5 kms from Banganga. **Ardh Kuwari** is 4.5 kms from Charan Paduka, where there is a 15-foot long cave called **Garbh Joon**, where the goddess hid herself. Located at a height of 4,800 feet, this cave is very narrow and the pilgrim has to crawl through it. **Sri Rama Temple** is near the Vaishno Devi cave, and **Bhairav Temple** is about 2.5 kms from the cave at a height of about 6,700 feet. Around 125 steps down below there is a **Shivalinga**. This is the place where Bhairav's head fell when the goddess killed him. A huge stone at the entrance of the cave represents his body .

☐☐☐

The Amarnath Cave is situated on the narrow openings between the mountains of Lidder Valley.

AMARNATH

It is said that Shiva made the gods immortal by providing them with nectar and upon their request resided here. The boon of immortality lent the name Amarnath.

According to legend, this is the cave where Shiva narrated the secret of immortality and the creation of universe to Goddess Parvati on Shravan Poornima—the full moon day in the month of August.

It is also believed that Kashyap Maharshi, the grandson of Brahma, destroyed the demons here and drained a big lake, Sati-Saras, named after Goddess Parvati. Bhrigu Maharshi was the first to have darshan of this holy cave.

Location

It is 13,700 feet above sea level in Jammu and Kashmir, 86 miles northeast of Srinagar. Surrounded by snow-clad mountains, the holy cave is 130 feet high. Shiva is worshipped here in the form of a Shivalinga-shaped ice block made by drops of water oozing naturally inside the cave. Behind an iron fence with an open gate, an underground trickle of water emerges 10 feet up from a small cleft in the sedimentary rock and freezes as it drops to form a tall, smooth cone of ice.

The Lingams

Most of the year, the cave is covered with snow. It is only accessible for a short period during summer. Thousands of Hindu pilgrims visit this cave, especially on the full moon day in August. At this time, the ice lingam reaches its largest size. During July-August, a pure white lingam forms in this cave. Water droplets trickle slowly from the top of the cave and freeze into ice when they fall. First, a solid base is formed and then the lingam gets formed from an ice stalagmite that waxes and wanes with the moon's cycle. By its side are two more ice lingams considered to be that of Goddess Parvati, the consort of Shiva, and their son Ganesha. The cave faces the south. Inside the Amarnath Cave, there is a small cave on the left of the image from which a chalk-like substance is given to pilgrims as vibhuti.

The Legend of Lord Shiva

Once the goddess asked her husband Shiva why and when he began wearing beads of skulls. Shiva told her that whenever she was reborn he would add one more skull to his beads. Thereupon, Parvati asked why she went through birth and death while he was immortal. She then wanted to know the secret of immortality. Shiva disclosed that his immortality was due to Amarkatha. But Parvati insisted on knowing the real reason.

Finally, Shiva agreed to disclose the *amar rahasya* or eternal truth about the secret of immortality. To impart this knowledge, he searched for a lonely place where no living creature could hear him. He then chose the Amarnath Cave. Shiva left his bull Nandi at Pahalgam. He released the moon from his hair at Chandanwari. The snakes around his neck were released on the banks of the lake Sheshnag. He left his son Ganesha at Mahagunas Parbat, also called Maha Ganesh Hill. The five elements—earth, water, air, fire and sky—controlled by Shiva, were left behind at Panchatarni.

Thereafter, Shiva and Parvati entered the cave. Lord Shiva sat on a deerskin and began to meditate. So that no living being could hear the tale, he created Rudra, named him Kalagni and ordered him to spread fire to ensure there was no living being in and around the holy cave. Then Lord Shiva began to narrate the secret of immortality to Parvati. But as a matter of chance, two pigeon eggs lying beneath the deerskin, on which Lord Shiva was seated, remained protected. Eggs were believed to be non-living and they were protected by Shiva's Asana. Due to the heat, the eggs hatched and the two pigeons listened to Shiva's narration quietly. Shiva had asked Parvati to be fully awake throughout the narration. But Parvati fell asleep midway.

At the end of his discourse, Parvati revealed that she had not listened to him fully since she fell asleep. The pigeons—which had heard the entire story of creation—now flew out of the cave.

The pair of pigeons which were born out of the eggs had listened to the secret of immortality (Amar Katha) so they became immortal.

Journey through Chandanwari and Panchatarni

Sheshnag Lake

Even today, pilgrims see pigeons inside the cave although the surroundings are full of ice and devoid of any creatures or vegetation.

The Legend of Buta Malik

According to another legend, a shepherd named Buta Malik discovered this holy cave. A saint gave Buta Malik a bagful of coal. When he reached home, he was surprised to find that the bag was full of gold coins. With great joy he went to the saint to thank him. But instead of the saint, he saw the holy cave and a Shivalinga. At once, he informed all the villagers.

Since then, this cave has become a sacred pilgrim spot. Even today, the descendents of Malik are given a percentage of the donations and the rest goes to the shrine's management.

The Pilgrimage

The yatra to Amarnath begins from either Srinagar (141 kms) or Pahalgam (44.8 kms). The confluence of the rivers **Sheshnag**

Journey via Baltal trek

and **Lidder** is located at Pahalgam, which is near the banks of Lidder River and 96 kms from Srinagar. From Pahalgam, the 45 km trek is covered in four days on an ancient route. The first major stop is at **Chandanwari**, where the rivers **Asthanmarg** and **Sheshnag** meet. The next stop is **Sheshnag**, a mountain that derives its name from its seven peaks resembling the seven heads of **Adisesha**. From here, one climbs to **Pissu Top**, where the gods are believed to have crushed demons. Further up is **Sheshnag Lake** at a height of about 12,000 feet and 12 kms from Chandanwari. Sheshnag River flows out of this lake. Then one reaches Wavjan, before the steep climb to Mahagunas Pass at 14,000 feet. The route to Mahagunas is full of rivulets, waterfalls, and springs. From here there is a downward slope leading to **Panchatarni**, a meadow at a height of 12,000 feet.

Finally, one reaches Amarnath. Taxis and jeeps go up till Chandanwari 16 kms from Pahalgam, from where it is a trekking route. Ponies and dandies are also available for pilgrims. Alongside the Lidder stream the trek is through a narrow lane. But from the top of Pissu Hill, the ascending trek is comparatively smooth till Sheshnag. The Mahagunas Pass after Sheshnag is the highest point on the trek at 4,276 metres. From here, it is a downward slope till Panchatarni and thereafter is a 6 km ascent to Amarnath Cave. After crossing a curve, one can see Amarnath Cave. This is the traditional route.

The new route via **Baltal** is only 15 kms long. But the road here is narrow and *kuchcha,* compared to the traditional route. There are also steep rises and falls. This route can be covered in one day. The two routes meet at a place called **Sangam** 4 kms short of the holy cave. Due to terrorist activities and for security reasons, the Amarnath Yatra was suspended from 1991. It has now been resumed.

□□□

This is Asia's most sacred mountain and also known as **Meru, Sumeru, Sushumna, Hemadri, Ratnasanu, Karnikachala, Amaradri, Deva Parbat, Gana Parbat,** and **Rajatadri.**

Mt. Kailash is considered **Swayambhu**—the self-created one.

MOUNT KAILASH

Legend says that when Shiva swallowed poison that appeared while churning the ocean, he went in search of a cool land and chose this place.

This mountain is also considered the earthly manifestation of the world pillar or spiritual centre of the universe—the mythical Mount Meru that is 84,000 miles high and around which everything revolves. It is believed its roots are in hell and its summit reaches heaven. Atop Meru resides Lord Shiva with his consort Goddess Parvati, children Ganesha, Subramanya (Kartikeya) and his Ganas. Lord Shiva—who wears a garland of skulls and bones and smears himself with ash—signifies the burning of lower desires.

Location

This is one of the highest, loveliest, most desolate places on earth. It stands in a remote corner of western Tibet, bordering western Nepal. It is the highest part of Tibet, which is called the Roof of the World. It is unique in that it rises from the highest point of the Tibetan plateau like the hub of a giant wheel. From the hub, four mighty rivers flow in four different directions like spokes radiating outward.

The mountain itself looks like a great symmetrical, domed temple coated with ice and snow. It is shining white, standing tall and dominating. Kailash is very beautiful and considered to be the staircase from which the gods descend to earth. Mt. Kailash was formed some 30 million years ago when the Himalayas were in the early stages of formation. The entire land surrounding Mt. Kailash is devoid of any vegetation. At a distance, however, one can see hills of various hues—rose, violet, and flaming orange. Except for a few small bands of nomadic herders, the empty plains are crossed only by winds. The weather is very cold and can be unpredictably treacherous.

Sacred Mountain

This 22,028-foot rock pyramid is most sacred for four important ancient religions of the world that consider this the place where the Divine has taken earthly form. Hindus, Tibetan Buddhists, Jains and the pre-Buddhist Bon religion consider it the centre of the world.

Hindus

For Hindus, it is the domain of Lord Shiva. On Mt. Kailash, one can see two hollows and from a particular angle, the ice-covered dome of Kailash appears like a skull with two large eyeholes peeping out.

Tibetan Buddhists

Tibetan Buddhists call this mountain **Kang Rimpoche**—*the precious one of the glacial snow*. They regard it as the dwelling place of **Demchog**, also known as **Chakrasamvara** and his consort, **Dorje Phagmo**. They worship this mountain as the abode of Samvara—the wrathful manifestation of Buddha. They also consider Kailash as Dharmapala. On stone, they inscribe *Om Mani Padme Hum—hail to the jewel of creation in the lotus*—and see it as the navel of the world. To them, Mt. Kailash also represents the terrestrial projection of cosmic *mandala*, **Dhyana Buddha** and **Bodhi Sattva**—the wheel of life.

Jains

For Jains it is **Ashta Pada**. This is the place where their first Teerthankara Adinath Rishabhanath gained Enlightenment and attained salvation. They visit Ashta Pada near the southern face of Kailash.

Mt. Kailash view from Deraphuck

Mt. Kailash—the sapphire-like look

Bons of Tibet

For the Bons of Tibet, an ancient pre-Buddhist belief, it is the nine-storey Swastika Mountain, the mystic soul of the entire region. It is here, they believe, that their founder Shanrab descended from heaven. Tibetan saint **Milarepa** spent several years meditating in a cave here. The followers of Bon call the mountain **Tiseh** and believe it to be the seat of the Sky Goddess **Sipaimen**. Unlike the Hindus, Buddhists and Jains, the Bons make an anti-clockwise pilgrimage around Mt. Kailash. This was formerly the spiritual centre of **Zhang Zhung**, the ancient Bon empire in western Tibet. A few claim that Guru Nanak meditated here.

Mt. Kailash view from Ashta Pada

Sutlej River

Indus River

The Four Rivers

From Mt. Kailash, the four rivers flow in the four cardinal directions. The **Indus**, flows north, the **Brahmaputra**, also called **Yarlung Tsangpo**, flows east, the **Karnali** flows south and the **Sutlej** flows west. **Teerthapuri**—70 kms west of Kailash—is on the banks of the Sutlej. There is a hot water spring here. It is believed that at this place the demon **Bhasmasura** was burnt to ashes. This area is full of red and white mountains. The ***Kalpavriksha*** tree is supposed to adorn the slopes of Kailash.

The south face of Mt. Kailash is described as **sapphire**, the east **crystal**, the west **ruby** and the north **gold**. The city of **Kubera** is located here.

□□□

Here, demon king Ravana is supposed to have meditated upon Shiva.

The Hindus believe that gods descend from heaven to bathe here. It is believed that Lord Brahma himself created Mansarovar to help Marichi, his son, and other sages bathe during winter, before worshipping Lord Shiva in tantrik ritual for 12 long years in order to please him. Sage Parasuram is said to have stayed in an ashram on a hill on the banks of Mansarovar.

Buddhists believe Queen Maya took a holy bath in this lake before giving birth to Lord Buddha.

The Mansarovar Lake, round like the sun, and the lower lake Rakshas Tal is shaped like a crescent moon, and both are said to represent the solar and lunar forces.

MANSAROVAR

Location

Sprawling below 25 miles south of Mt. Kailash, and at its base, is the sacred Mansarovar. Located at a height of 14,930 feet above sea level, a 6-km long natural channel called Gangachhu connects Mansarovar with Rakshas Tal. Considered one of the highest fresh water lakes in the world, Tibetans call it **Maphamyumetreso** or **Victorious Lake**. This giant lake is of shifting colours. It is believed that Brahma the Creator had an insight for creation of this lake. With a circumference of 88 kms and a depth of 90 metres, the water area is 412 sq kms. The lake melts only in spring.

The Holy Dip

Taking a dip in this holy lake is believed to cure all diseases of body and mind. Hindus believe that a sacred bath here will help them attain salvation. Its water is said to possess miraculous healing powers. The Mansarovar Lake is closely surrounded by snow-clad peaks, which melt and fill the lake with chilled water.

Kailash-Mansarovar Tours

Almost all major passes of Uttaranchal Himalayas lead to Kailash-Mansarovar. Since 1981, under the auspices of the Ministry of External Affairs, Government of India, and with the co-operation of the Chinese Government, the **Kumaon Mandal Vikas Nigam** arranges trips to Kailash-Mansarovar via the **Lipulekh Pass**. In addition, various tour operators now organise trips. However, the pilgrimage was stopped when the Chinese Army entered Tibet. The Sino-Indian border clashes in 1959 had also sealed off all routes to Kailash-Mansarovar for a few years. But now, around 200 pilgrims are allowed to visit Kailash-Mansarovar every year.

For this trip, one has to go via the Ministry of External Affairs, which organises pilgrimages from June to September. On the basis of a draw, only a limited number are selected from among the thousands who apply. For the final selection, one has to be 18 years of age and medically fit to undertake the strenuous trip that requires almost 20,000 feet of trekking. This done, the visa and exchange formalities come next. The expenses per person are quite high—over US$2000, as a certain amount goes to the Chinese authorities to cover expenses of accommodation, transportation and other arrangements for the 15 days' duration of the trek.

Private Tours

Private tour operators take a tour from Kathmandu. Their representative organisations are also located in India. They take pilgrims by cars to Mansarovar and Kailash from the base camp at Darchen driving via the Tibetan Plateau. The road journey from Kathmandu is about five days to reach the base camp at Darchen, a small town located at the base of Mt. Kailash in Tibet. Tour operators cover a large part of Kailash-Mansarovar on jeeps.

Three Routes

There are three possible routes to reach Mt.Kailash from India. The official northern trekking route is via Uttaranchal up to the Lipulekh Pass. The Indian Government organises these tours. This is the oldest and longest route that involves trekking of

Rakshas Tal

Dolma Pass

Gouri Kund

around 300 kms. The second is by air to Kathmandu and from there by road to Lake Mansarovar and the base of Kailash, which covers a distance of 990 kms. The third is a shorter helicopter route to Kailash from Lhasa. Indian citizens must have a valid passport for this yatra.

The Pilgrimage

In the tour organised by the government, there are usually 16 batches of 35–60 pilgrims each. The first three days are spent in travelling by bus from Delhi. On the fourth day, the trek begins. En route, higher up towards the northwest, one can see the entrance to a cave believed to be that of Sage Vyasa. There is no vegetation beyond **Nabhidang**. Towards the east of this place lies **Om Parbat**. The base camp for Parikrama is **Darchen**. From here, the pilgrims of Kailash proceed to **Dolma Pass**. Immediately after crossing Dolma, there is a lake with greenish colour, **Gouri Kund**. Legend says that Goddess Parvati bathes here.

From Darchen the south side of Kailash can be seen, fully covered with ice. The southern face displays the markings of celestial steps, which are long vertical clefts punctuated by a horizontal line of rock strata.

Kailash Pradakshina

After reaching **Darchen**, pilgrims start their 32-mile parikrama around the sacred Kailash that looks like a huge Shivalinga. **Gouri Kund** on the parikrama route is one of the highest ponds in the world at 1,900 metres. To go around Kailash once, the 5 km **Kailash pradakshina** takes nearly 3 to 5 days. One single pradakshina erases the accumulated sins of a lifetime, while 108 circuits enable one to achieve **salvation** or ***Nirvana***.

□□□

Baisakhi
Basant Panchami
Bihu
Chhath Puja
Diwali
Durga Puja
Dussehra
Ganesh Chaturthi
Gangaur
Nanak Jayanti
Holi
Janmashtami
Karva Chauth
Lohri
Mahashivratri
Mahavir Jayanti
Makar Sankranti
Naag Panchami
Navreh
Onam
Pongal
Raksha Bandhan
Ram Navami
Puri Rathyatra
Teej
Ugadi
Vishu

HINDOOLOGY BOOKS
An imprint of **Pustak Mahal**

S.P. Sharma & Seema Gupta • Size: 8.25″X10.5″ Pages:148 (H.B.)
Fully Illustrated in colour